Massive

Brutalism Now and Then

Expressive

Sculptural

Massive

Chris van Uffelen

Brutalism Now and Then

Expressive

Sculptural

BRAUN

Brutalism Now and Then

Brutalism is back. Probably the most misunderstood architectural term of all time is making a comeback and is no longer the specter of things long gone. It is also growing in popularity in non-expert circles. What was presented in films like *Clockwork Orange* by Stanley Kubrick (1971) and in books such as *High Rise* by H. G. Ballard (1975) as the stage for an uncivilized and violent society, is slowly once more taking its place in popular culture.

Was this architectural style, typical of the 1960s and 1970s, really brutal and was this even its intention? The answer, by and large, is "no". It was Post-Modernism during the 1970s and 1980s that first associated the term with such characteristics, in order to separate its own trends from those of the previous generation of architecture and to further its quest to appear more civilized in comparison.

It is no longer possible to accurately determine exactly where the term "Brutalism" originated from, but there are nevertheless several founding legends. It most probably began when Hans Asplund referred to the Villa Göth in Uppsala, built by the architects Bengt Edman and Lennart Holm, as an example of "nybrutalism" (Neo-Brutalism), combining this most useless of prefixes with "ism" in an attempt to poke fun at it. At the beginning of the 1950s, Scandinavian architecture was highly popular in England and the term was soon adopted by English architects, and also by Reyner Banham, one of the most influential art historians and critics of the time. He published the article "The New Brutalism" in the September edition of Architectural Review in 1955 and even had the appropriate architecture at hand to use as an example.

The Hunstanton School in Norfolk, built by Alison and Peter Smithson between 1949 and 1954, was intended to be one of the first true representatives of the new Brutalism style. This is an imposing construction, the proportions and appearance of which were strongly influenced by the architecture of Ludwig Mies van der Rohe. The exposed steel frame is filled with brick and glass and the technical installations have been left visible. The visibility of the pipes and integrated building technology was initially a typical defining criterion for brutalist architecture, but the even more important criterion of exposed concrete is missing. However, the names of the two architects provided a second reference to the term Brutalism; Peter Smithson was nicknamed "Brutus" by his fellow students: Brut + Alis(on) + m = Brutalism. The use of exposed concrete that characterized so many brutalist buildings presented the third criterion for a true definition of the term. In French, this material is called béton brut, and was the visible raw concrete that Le Corbusier propagated as a surface material with his design of the Unité d'Habitation. It was also Le Corbusier who introduced the non-orthogonal shape of sculptural undulating concrete that influenced the design of so many buildings over the next few years. Mies van der Rohe and Le Corbusier served Banham as two worthy predecessors of his new architecture, despite the fact that he positioned himself against Mies van der Rohe's lightweight architectural esthetic. Ultimately, the word "brutal" stands in contrast to the elegant glass and steel buildings seen in miesian postwar Functionalism. Béton brut also offered an analogy to Jean Dubuffet's Art Brut, where Banham recognized the same style of "direct expression" seen in the artwork of Jackson Pollock. When Banham's book, also called *The New Brutalism*, appeared in 1966 in both German (published by the Karl Krämer Verlag) and in English (by the Architectural Press) brutalist buildings had increased significantly in popularity – not least due to the involvement of Team Ten architects, Structuralism in the Netherlands and Metabolism in Japan. Apart from the Smithsons and the architects of the London County Council architecture departments (a nucleus of Brutalism), Aldo van Eyck, Atelier 5, Kiyonori Kikutake, Walter Förderer, Louis I. Kahn and Paul Rudolph are shown with examples of their architecture.

Peter and Alison Smithson, Secondary School, Hunstanton, 1954 Reyner Banhams starting point of Brutalism.

Within the pages of this book, these historical buildings are presented between the modern examples so that the reader is able to gain their own impression of similarities and differences. However, this is not about presenting the entire spectrum of postwar buildings, but rather the examples that best typify the style. The five detailed chapter introductions can be analyzed to find a number of common themes and departures, ultimately leading to a deeper understanding of "Brutalism now and then".

ROZHLAS A TELEVÍZIA SLOVENSKA

CHAPTER 1

Material as Found

Concrete
Brick
Steel
Wood
Glass

Béton brut – exposed concrete – this is generally seen as being synonymous with Brutalism, at least when critics have gotten over their tendency to categorize the style as aggressive towards those using the buildings. On the one hand, one of Reyner Banham's intentions was to include violence and aggression in the terms he used, but more in the sense of the powerful impression left by the buildings than their oppressive intention. On the other hand, it is not only the concrete that was supposed to express the "brut" – French for "raw" – and untreated aspects of the style. Brutalism is much more concerned with presenting materials "as found", as Banham put it, or using raw-looking variations of all the materials selected.

In 1966 Banham stated on page 68 of his book *The New Brutalism:* "… an architecture whose concepts of order were as far removed from those of 'architectural composition' as those of Pollock were removed from the routines of painterly composition (i.e. balance, congruence or contrast of forms within a dominant rectangular formal – we argued much whether Pollock paid any regard to the edges of the canvas when dribbling his action paintings); an architecture as uninhibited in its response to the nature of materials 'as found', as were the Composers of 'musique concrete' in their response to natural sounds 'as recorded'." In 1953, Robert and Alison Smithson held an exhibition and published a catalogue, together with Eduardo Paolozzi and Nigel Henderson, both entitled *Parallel of Life and Art*. This sought to portray not only the anti-esthetic but also violence as anti-art in the sense of Art Brut.

The French "brut" and English "brutal" meant, at least in terms of architecture, that the concrete should not be hidden, wood not sanded, plaster not smoothed, paint not applied directly to the walls, and that brick should retain

its rough surface. Highly processed materials such as metal and glass were forced into the background.

Trendy skyscrapers of steel and glass were the epitome of modern architecture: the Lever House in New York City, NY, 1950–1952 designed by Gordon Bunshaft and Natalie de Blois from the office of Skidmore, Owings and Merrill (SOM) was considered to be the ideal example that many other buildings should follow. Ludwig Mies van der Rohe also supported this ideal. In 1919 he designed a glass tower for Berlin, inspired by the glass house ideal propagated by the German Expressionists

Claude Parent and Paul Virilio, Sainte-Bernadette-du-Banlay, Nevers 1968
The monolithic concrete block is inspired by the architecture of German bunkers.

Page 12: Štefan Svetko, Štefan Ďurkovič and Barnabáš Kissling, Building of Slovak radio, Bratislava, 1983
Metal pyramid upside down.

(Paul Scheerbart, Bruno Taut), although the tower was never actually built. In terms of its delicate appearance, the skeleton of this design surpassed (at least in the sketches) the existing technical capabilities, even in 1955 or 1966. After emigrating to America, he built a strikingly delicate bungalow, Farnsworth House near Plano, IL between 1949 and 1951: the concrete panels are barely noticeable between the steel elements and the glass. He also built a glass high-rise similar to that built by SOM. The Seagram Building in New York had a less delicate appearance and is more rigorous in terms of form than the Berlin design. In comparison to these thin-skinned buildings, Brutalism with its elephant skin suddenly erupted onto the architectural scene, banishing all sense of the elegant modesty that

Le Corbusier, Palace of Assembly, Chandigarh, 1962
In-situ concrete in curvilinear forms need accurate working carpenters.

had characterized the previous style. But Mies van der Rohe also proved himself to be a master of concrete: his Promontory Apartments, built in South Shore in 1949, clearly show a concrete skeleton, and his Research Foundation Mechanical Engineering Building at the Illinois Institute of Technology, built in 1952 (both located in Chicago), demonstrate an obvious brick infill, enabling Banham to name Mies van der Rohe as a predecessor of Brutalism, despite the fact that his most famous buildings are exactly the opposite of this. Banham named the Hunstanton School in Norfolk, designed by the Smithsons between 1949 and 1954, as the first brutalist building. This also invoked the brutalist buildings by Mies van der Rohe. The Hunstanton School building has got a steel skeleton that has been filled in with brick – so much for béton brut.

Brick also played a very important role in Brutalism. Banham uses the Gut Garkau building in north-east Germany by Hugo Häring as an example of this. Built between 1922 and 1928, the built construction is just a small part of the original extensive design. The floor plates punch through the façade and are visible as concrete bands supporting rough brick walls. Even the timber walls are rough. This motif of making the structural elements visible on the façade can also be seen in work by the Amsterdam School, and in the work of Hendrik Petrus Berlage in Amsterdam, where huge flat brick walls come into play (Beurs, 1899 – 1903). Both motifs were adopted in the Netherlands in Brick Functionalism by "De 8" (Benjamin Merkelbach, Ch. J. F. Karsten AVRO-Studio, Hilversum, 1936) and remained in fashion until after the postwar era. Both flat walls and concrete bands can also be seen in Le Corbusier's Maisons Jaoul in Neuilly-sur-Seine from 1956, although Banham claimed in 1966 on page 125 that they

Kenzo Tange, Press and Broadcaster Center, Shizuoka, 1967
13 prefabricated cantilevered glass and steel boxes in five groups were connected asymmetrically to the central beam.

had "a concept of plan, space and geometry that has nothing in common with any of the Brutalist buildings that use brick in any related manner." On page 85, he did however admit that, "The steel and glass of Hunstanton, even when allied to the rough imagery of 'Parallel of Life and Art' seemed too thin, too elegant to fulfil the implications of violence and crudity carried by the word 'brutal'. Then came the Maisons Jaoul in 1956, and the vacuum of architectural meaning was dramatically filled. The later history of New Brutalism has much less to do with the theoretical propositions of the Smithsons than it has to do with the progress and permutations of the style invented by Le Corbusier for these houses on one podium at Neuilly." The curving roof designs do however create an "image" – a further demand from Banham that will be considered in the next chapter.

James Stirling – who later became a protagonist of Post-Modernism – claimed to have been shocked by these buildings, and said that they directly influenced the design for the Langham Close Flats, in Ham Common, London, built together with James Gowan from 1955 to 1958. But this ensemble clearly shows Dutch Brick Functionalism from the 1930s. Ultimately, it was probably the Scandinavian relationship to English Brutalism that made brick so popular. Like Häring's Gut Garkau, Alvar Alto's Community Center in Säynätsalo (1950–1952) also demonstrated the use of brick and wood that emphasized both a rural and local connection. The New Empiricism or New Humanism seen in the work of Sven Markelius or Ralph Erskin sought to provide life's essentials in the form of simple and functional residential buildings. This usually resulted in a calm and unobtrusive Functionalism.

In the case of Brutalism, brick gained a certain dramatic edge, using the reds and oranges seen in Expressionism, the pinks and yellows of Functionalism, and the

Paul Rudolph, University Chapel Tuskegee, AL, 1969
This building has large expressive brick walls.

browns of more traditional architecture. Bricks are versatile and can be irregular in color or show different nuances from one brick to the next, although they are seldom whitewashed or sintered. Bricks can be irregular in terms of shape or perfectly formed – as often seen in Functionalism. Brick walls are often straight rather than curved, as this would demand more skill, form a grid or pattern, or are located in front of or behind the line of the brick.

Natural stone was also used in Brutalism, with an even more dramatic effect. This is often overlooked, but can be found on countless exposed aggregate concrete buildings, where the river pebbles have been washed to the surface. This is a popular aggregate due to the variety of colors and the esthetically pleasing results. Other stones were also used, washed to the surface of the poured concrete or chiseled from the set concrete (bush-hammering), creating an impression similar to that achieved by the use of gabions today.
Marble only rarely makes an appearance. The polished stone seen in the work of Mies van der Rohe and the Art Deco is by definition rather "un-brut". Where marble is used, for example in the Kulturhaus in Wolfsburg by Alvar Alto (1958–1962), it almost seems inappropriate on the heavy, closed building volume. Even the more "as found" material of Norwegian limestone seen in the Mainz City Hall by Arne Jacobson and Otto Weitling (1968–1974) is almost too homogenous in appearance to really be brut. The use of natural stone in Brutalism seeks a more rustic style, as seen in Frank Lloyd Wright's Second Jacobs House in 1948, or his Usonian Houses, which simply ooze charm. The wood in these designs is also used "as found", with a clearly visible grain. The archaic block huts with rough timber and heavy beams suited the brutalist style, but not the marble-clad palace esthetic.

Le Corbusier, Maisons Jaoul, Neuilly-sur-Seine, 1956
The pair of houses feature a rugged esthetic of unpainted cast concrete béton brut and roughly detailed brickwork.

A further possible example would be the sue of embossed stones – like the ones Banham showed with the Church of the Madonna det Poveri in Milan by Luigi Figini and Gino Pollini, 1956 – but this was seldom used. The usage of natural stone and wood clearly shows Marc Antoine Laugier's (1753) "primitive hut" ideal of Brutalism that Kenneth Frampton mentions in *Modern Architecture: A critical history* (1990, p. 265) and puts the Brutalism in a romantic tradition. However, Brutalism was forced to consider one shiny material – namely glass. Industrial materials such as glass and steel both proved problematic in terms of their nature-bound esthetics. While it was possible to choose less precious metals than steel for the façade – with a patina or corroded surface, as demonstrated by the Slovak Radio building in Bratislava by Štefan Svetko, Štefan Ďurkovič and Barnabáš Kissling (1967–1983), glass "as found" is simply sand. However, there are ways of making glass appear archaic, for example by using flawed glass with air bubbles or panels that are not flat. Hand-crafted glass was used in the construction of the Nová scéna by Karel Prager in Prague. In 1983, Stanislav Libenský suggested that this building could be enveloped with 4,000 blown glass bricks. This move was intended to draw attention to the Bohemian glass industry. In the pilgrimage church Notre Dame du Haut in Ronchamp (1950–1955), Le Corbusier also targeted the archaic esthetic, both by painting the glass panes and by implementing a technique from the 1930s, Dalle de verre, that uses pieces of colored glass set in a matrix of concrete and epoxy resin or other supporting material. This technique was also used between 1959 and 1961 during the construction of the Berlin Memorial Church by Egon Eiermann, where 16,000 glass mosaic elements by the French artists Gabriel Loire were incorporated into the octagon of the church building.

The ultimate in terms of material was exposed concrete, "to produce an architectural surface of

Karel Prager, Nová scéna Prague, 1983
The unique use of over 4000 diversely shaped glass tiles makes the whole building an original sculptural work of art.

a rugged grandeur that seems to echo that of the well-weathered Doric columns of temples in Magia Graecia" as Banham says in 1966 on page 16 discussing Ronchamp, most archaic is concrete either as exposed aggregate concrete with natural aggregate or bush-hammered. The first buildings to be built using exposed concrete were constructed in the early 20th century, but techniques were used to disguise this and imitate other materials. François Hennebique added false joins to the concrete façade of his own house in Bourg-la-Reine, 1899–1902, imitating brick. One early exposed aggregate building stands out: Frank Lloyd Wright's Unity Temple in Oak Park, IL, was built as early as 1905 to 1908. Later, it was August Perret who first began to explore the esthetic potential of this new material, and his Notre-Dame in Raincy (1922–1923) has impressions left from the formwork in the less visible areas. The Musée des Travaux Publics in Paris, 1936–1938, shows the impressions left from the areas where the formwork boards met. Almost all the iconic buildings from the Classical Modern era covered the concrete with plaster. Le Corbusier was the first to use the impressions left by the wooden formwork as an esthetic element. During his speech at the handover he emphasized, "the smallest irregularities can be seen in the concrete from the formwork: the joints between the boards, the wood fibers, the knots in the wood." When concrete is poured into the formwork, the finer materials travel up to the surface and are visible on the surface when the concrete is dry. This gave the concrete a natural aspect – similar to the aggregate visible in exposed aggregate concrete. Even large surfaces gained a unique and more lively appearance – even though the impressions were often repeated due to the reuse of the boards. Ultimately, these carpentered formworks became too expensive and were no longer used. They were replaced by large industrial formwork elements – the beginning of the end for béton brut in the 1980s.

Karel Prager, Jiří Kadeřábek and Jiří Albrecht, former Parliament Building, Prague, 1973 This extraordinary superstructure once housed the Czechoslovak parliament. In 2009 it became part of the National Museum.

Furthermore, in-situ concrete – in contrast to prefabricated elements – became problematic in terms of maintenance, usually due to sloppy work carried out on site. But after becoming nearly extinct during the 1980s, exposed concrete became popular once more during the 1990s – initially not in the Brutalist style, but painted, sanded and even polished (Morger, Degelo and Kerenz: Kunstmuseum Liechtenstein in Vaduz, 1998–2000). Since the turn of the century, raw concrete has also made something of a comeback, sometimes as exposed aggregate concrete, but more often bush-hammered (Mexican Embassy in Berlin by Teodoro González de León and Francisco Serrano, 1999–2001). Over the last five to ten years, imprints left by the formwork have become a feature once more, patterns like of the Unité d'Habitation in Marseille, 1947–1952, raw wood with a visible grain, have become more popular, although these are caused by industrial plastic matrixes put in the framework rather than by natural materials.

BOSTON CITY HALL

Gerhard Kallmann, McKinnel & Knowles, Boston City Hall, 1968
Rough béton brut.

by Wespi de Meuron Romeo Architects

Concrete House in Füllinsdorf

This newly built residential house is located in a quarter characterized by older single-family houses in the village of Füllinsdorf. The area is intended for further development in the future, so this house has been positioned on the lower half of the plot to allow for the possible construction of a second house in the future. The design is reserved and elegant, allowing it to blend into its surroundings. The main entrance is located on the lower floor, facing the valley. A second entrance is positioned on the upper level, where visitors can enter the main living area via a small courtyard. In the living areas, the exterior walls next to the fireplace house various niches for books and art objects. The house is characterized by a rather archaic design vocabulary that makes use of just a few different materials.

Location: Füllinsdorf, Switzerland
Architect: Wespi de Meuron Romeo Architects
Year of Completion: 2015

Elevation

Section

Covered terrace with washed concrete

Exterior with various kinds of concrete

Massive door opening

Fitted kitchen

Windows and niches in random positions

Le Corbusier's chaise longue LC4 in living area

by Fránek Architects

CCC Gallery

The CCC is a gallery and villa in Beijing, belonging to a married couple – painters who live in the city. The building is located in a rapidly developing district, characterized by a high volume of artists. The project brief for the narrow site initially involved designing the building's main façade. During the course of work on the project, this brief increased to include the whole building. This three-story building now comprises technical facilities, studios for rent, a flat, and the owner's studio. The structure of the building is typical of Chinese historical buildings and is centered around an atrium. An opening in the main façade has been made according to the principles of Feng Shui and is intended to bring affluence and prosperity.

Location: Beijing, China
Architect: Fránek Architects
Year of Completion: 2010

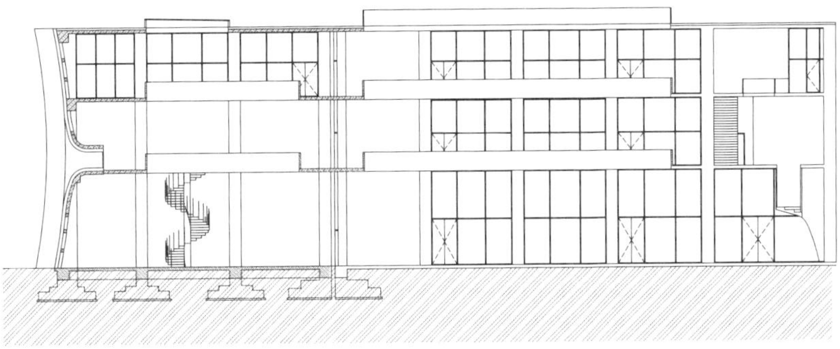

Section

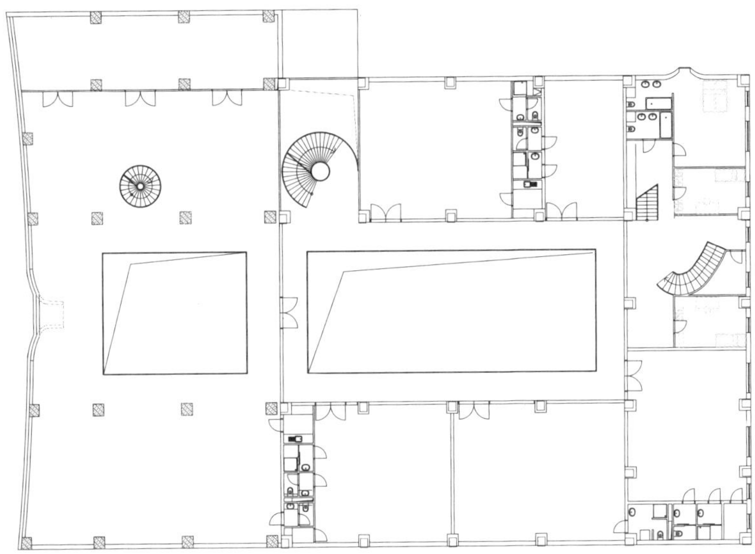

Second floor plan

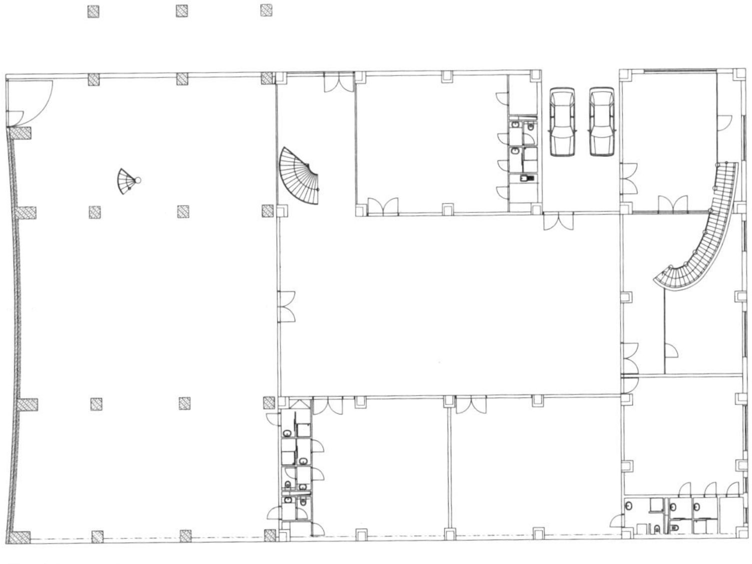

First floor plan

Glass front contrasts concrete exterior

Gallery interior

Spiral staircase inside

Round opening from inside

Round opening from outside

by Fritz Wotruba

Wotruba Church

152 raw concrete blocks of varying size and apparently arranged at random with no sense of symmetry – for this design, sculptor Fritz Wotruba combined architecture and sculpture. In his own words he says of the cyclops-like religious building that he wished to "design something that shows that being poor does not have to be ugly, and abstinence can take place in an environment that can be beautiful and make you happy despite its perceived simplicity." The interior is also characterized by the horizontal, vertical and angled blocks. The altar wall consists of a vertical block. The light falls through irregular openings, creating a dynamic lighting effect with overlapping bundles of light. Access to the church is via a generously glazed entrance area.

Location: Vienna, Austria
Architect: Fritz Wotruba
Year of Completion: 1976

Glass and concrete detail

Interior

Entrance area

by Menis Arquitectos

Holy Redeemer Church

A visual reference within the poorly designed neighborhood, the church has an impressive appearance, with the four independent volumes rising up as large rocks in the landscape. Between them, narrow spaces act like patios, allowing air and light to circulate. Natural light filters through the cracks, revealing the rough textures of the concrete and giving a sense of mystic presence. Balancing the proportions of the voids and the surrounding built environment was vital for developing the identity of the project. Concrete has been used to ensure energy efficiency and this characteristic is optimized by the thermal insulation of the walls. Acoustics are controlled with irregular surfaces, be it textured concrete or volcanic stones. When approaching a surrounding ramp provides access to the square and to the second floor, thus solving the issue of the steep topography.

Location: Santa Cruz de Tenerife, Spain
Architect: Menis Arquitectos
Year of Completion: 2017

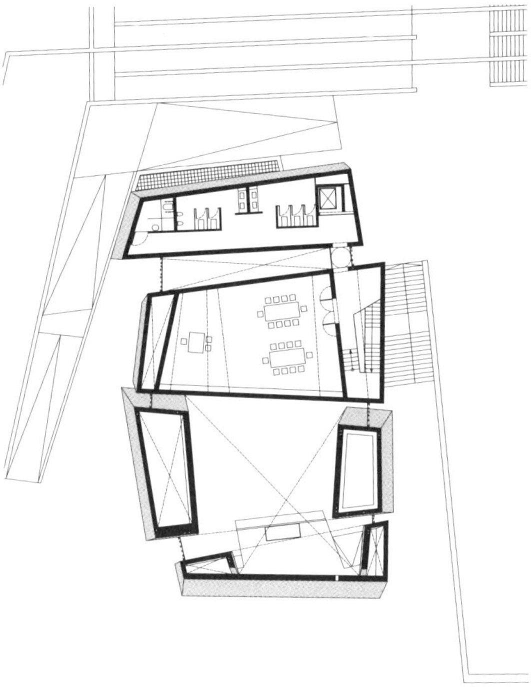

Second floor

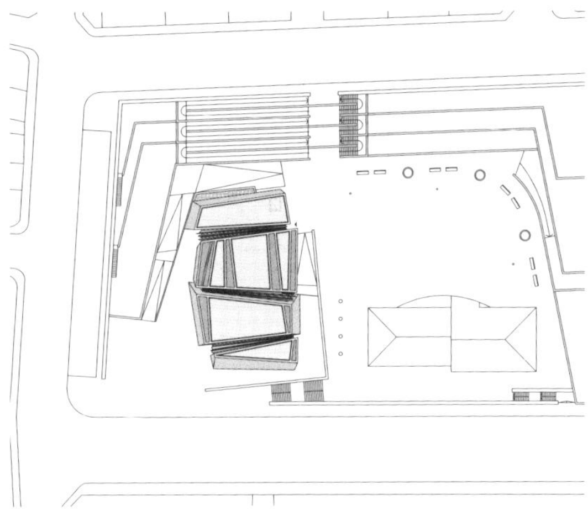

Site plan

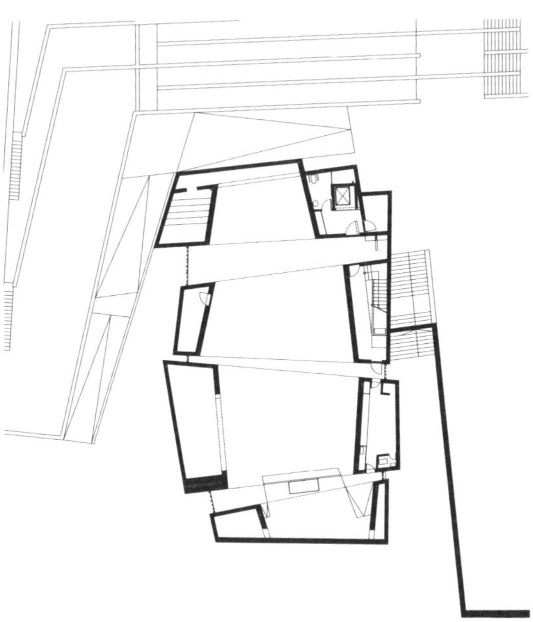

Ground floor

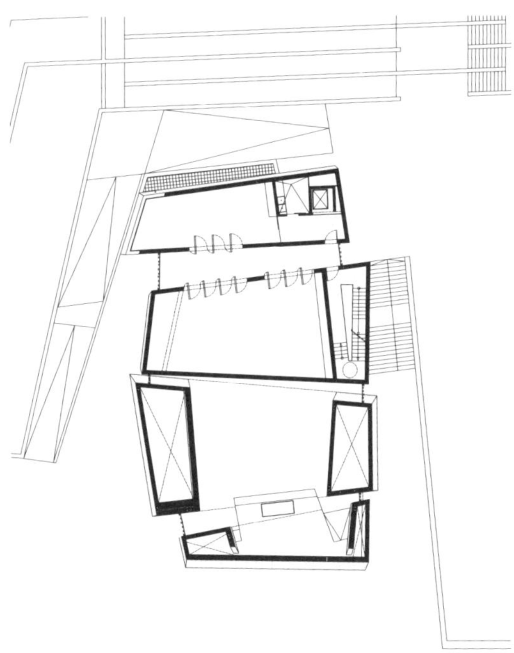

First floor

Bird's-eye view of the church and social center

Rough textures

A sense of mystic presence

Library in the social center of the church

Natural light filters through crosscut in the façade

by Cheng Design

House 6 Menlo Park

This house is a hybrid structure comprising a monolithic concrete core and traditional wood framing, traditional rough, board-formed concrete walls and hyper-smooth concrete walls, articulated with bands of exposed aggregate. Family communal life occurs in the concrete structure of the main living core while private life occurs in the wood-framed wings. The concept was to create a building that, while minimalist, would convey integral tactile design and craft throughout by controlling the mixed design of the concrete walls. The concrete walls were poured using a formwork-reducing slip-cast technique. The panels were grouped together in single-height "lifts". With each lift came the ability to control how the concrete was performing. Reaching into the forms added subtle bands of color and prevented any marring of the glossy forms.

Location: Menlo Park, CA, USA
Architect: Cheng Design
Year of Completion: 2007

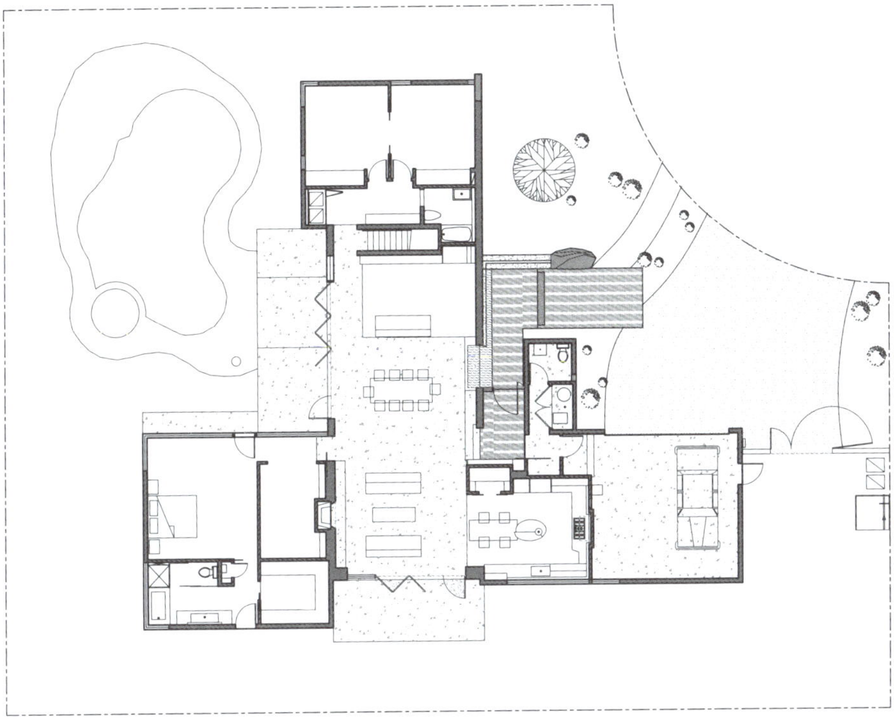

Ground floor plan

Entrance with view of the dining area

Artist-made light installation in the dining area

Concrete wall in the entrance area

Concrete, steel, wood, and bamboo

Japanese plastered wall leading to the main living area

The complex as massive sculpture of concrete and wood

by Erno Goldfinger

Trellick Tower

This 98-meter tall residential tower is considered to be one of the world's most important examples of Brutalism. The most characteristic feature is the division into a service tower and a narrow high-rise residential tower. The façade of the service tower is dominated by slim windows with a staggered arrangement. At the top of the tower is an entirely glazed room that once functioned as a heating room. The façade of the main building comprises exposed aggregate concrete plates. Balconies of varying lengths give the tower a graphic pattern of rectangles, similar to Le Corbusier's Unité d'Habitation. Both of the buildings are connected with each other via ten skyways. When it was built, the 31-story high-rise was England's highest residential tower and it remains one of London's landmark buildings.

Location: London, England
Architect: Erno Goldfinger
Year of Completion: 1972

Reception and lobby

Main volume and service tower

Access skywalks

by BAK arquitectos

BB House

This plot, located in the forest of Mar Azul, is uneven in relation to the two surrounding streets. While this complicates the provision of access to the site, it has the advantage of protecting the house from the gazes of passersby. The client requested a three-bedroom house, designed not only for summer use, but also on other occasions throughout the year. A large kitchen was required with generous outdoor expansions. Using a ladder hidden in the dune's natural slope, the building is accessed through a main terrace that develops along the longest side, so that by opening the sliding doors full integration is achieved between the indoor and the outdoor. The house has been constructed using three basic materials: exposed concrete, glass and pine wood tables and beams.

Location: Mar Azul, Buenos Aires Province, Argentina
Architects: BAK arquitectos / Besonías-Kruk
Year of Completion: 2011

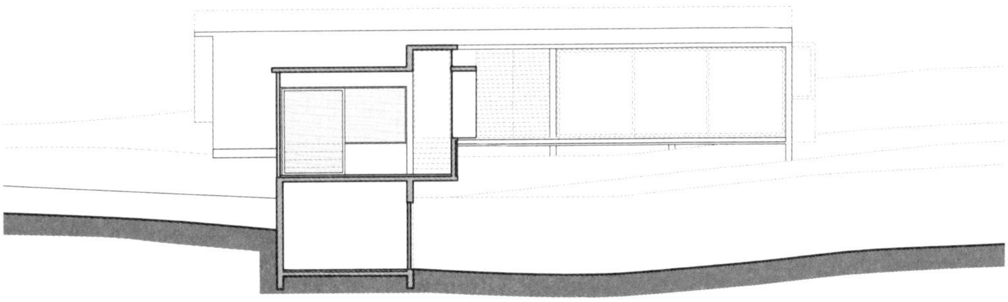

Longitudinal section

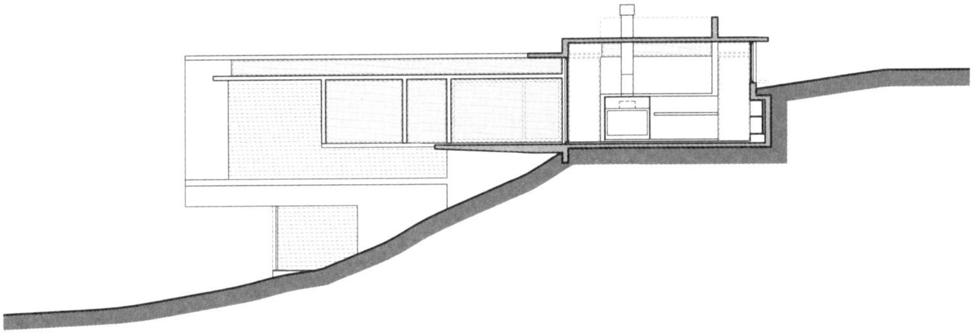

Cross section

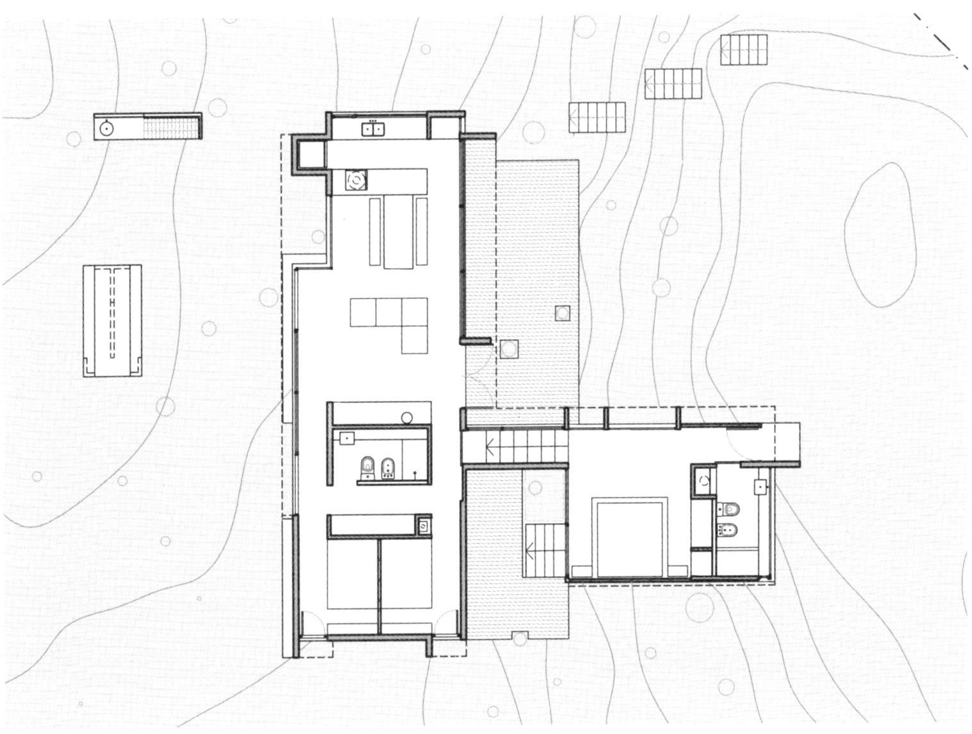

Floor plan

Northwest view

Northeast view

South façade

North façade

Integrated kitchen area

Entrance deck

by Foldes Architects

Volcano Park Visitor Center

The iconic Kemenes Volcano Park Visitor Center in Hungary is located 200 kilometers to the west of Budapest, and was built as the result of a national architectural contest announced in 2009 by the Celldömölk City Council and won by Foldes Architects. Upon entering the building, the visitor is met by two engaging attractions. The vertically open space first captures the eye. Five floors above, a small window lets in a beam of light, symbolizing the "eruption" point on the flat roof. On the opposite side, the industrial materials of the façade appear consistent with the interior: naked concrete walls, dark gray resin flooring, steel staircase and corridor, and the corten steel cubes that are also visible from the outside. The varied height and location of bridges link the different sizes and positions of the corten boxes.

Location: Celldömölk, Hungary
Architect: Foldes Architects
Year of Completion: 2013

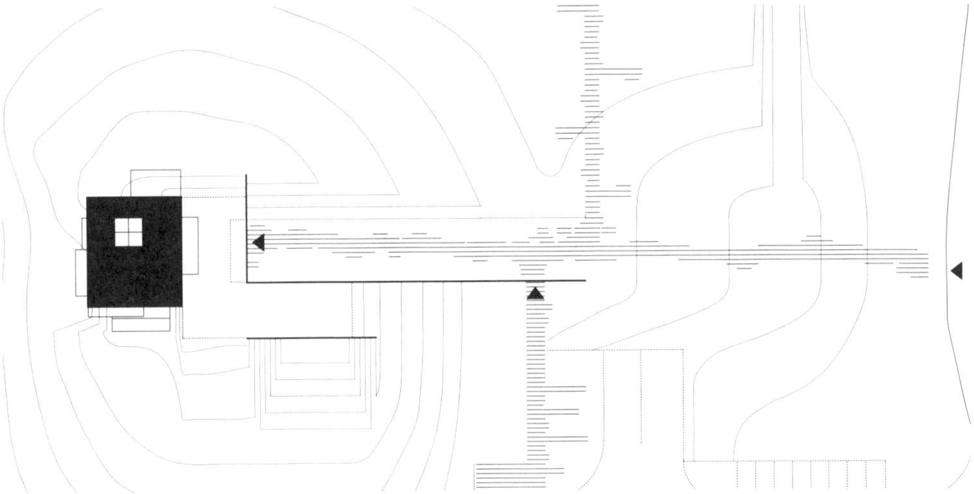

Site plan

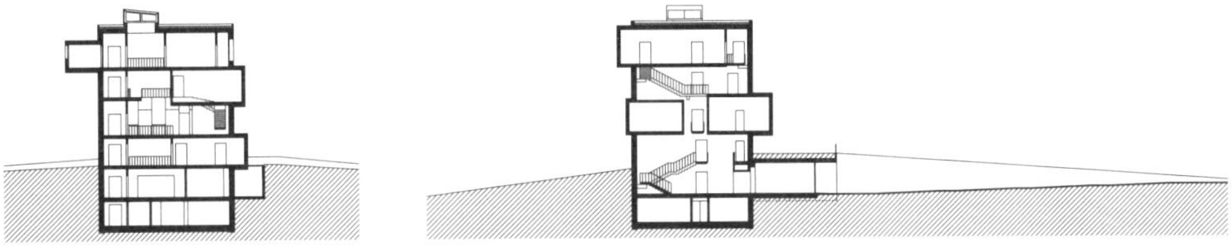

Sections

Ground floor to fourth floor plan

Ság hill lookout on the west side

Interior of tower area

Stairwell

Exterior view

Detail of materials

Worm's-eye view of open interior space

by Clorindo Testa, Francisco Bullrich, Alicia Cazzaniga

National Library

The National Library in Buenos Aires is the largest library in Argentina. As a symbol of industry and new technology, this building establishes clearly defined spaces with an outside public plaza and entrance on the ground floor. The brutalist design is characterized by maximizing the open space on the ground floor with a public park. The reading room was placed on the upper floor with views towards the city, the book archives are located underground in the cellar. The idea of strength inspires the entire design. The strong and powerful volume lifts the reading rooms using four concrete cores, each with 13 piles above the ground. The building looks like a monumental table and this emblematic work has become an example of iconic contemporary architecture in Argentina.

Location: Buenos Aires, Argentina
Architect: Clorindo Testa, Francisco Bullrich, Alicia Cazzaniga
Year of Completion: 1992

Building in context

Concrete gives the building a monumental appearance

by studio inches architettura

MeCrì Museum Pavilion

This museum extension was planned in 2012 and realized in 2016. The intervention not only leaves the existing stone walls (protected by regional law) untouched, it also creates a dialogue with them, through materiality and by recalling their existing height and length. As the old stone walls degrade through time, the new concrete boundaries will stand in their place. The exposed aggregate concrete creates a finish that is well integrated into the context. The walls of the intervention define an inner courtyard that connects the two parts of the MeCrì Museum. The new exhibition room is covered by a pitched roof that is integrated into its surroundings thanks to its form and materiality. A nine-meter skylight crowns the roof and creates a mystic atmosphere in the pavilion interior. The monolithic mass of the roof is strengthened by the use of local stone as cladding.

Location: Via Mondacce, Switzerland
Architect: studio inches architettura
Year of Completion: 2016

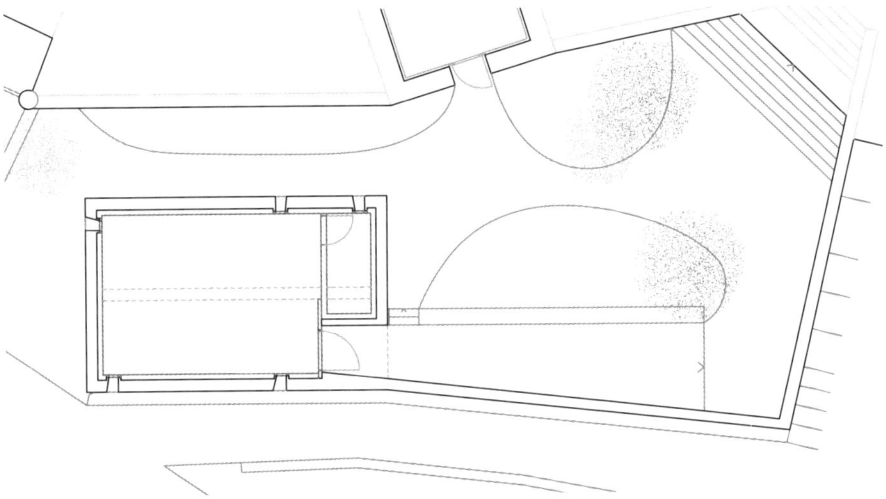

Plan

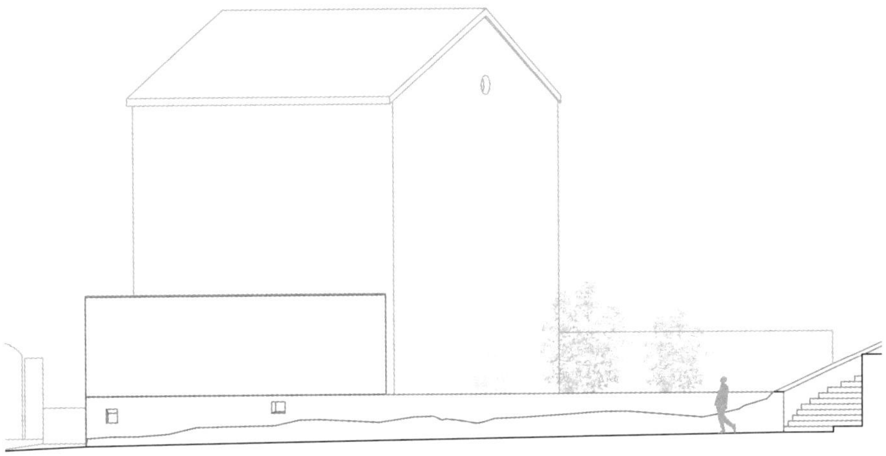

East elevation

Section

Exterior view from public path

Exterior street view

Exposed aggregate walls

Mystic atmosphere inside

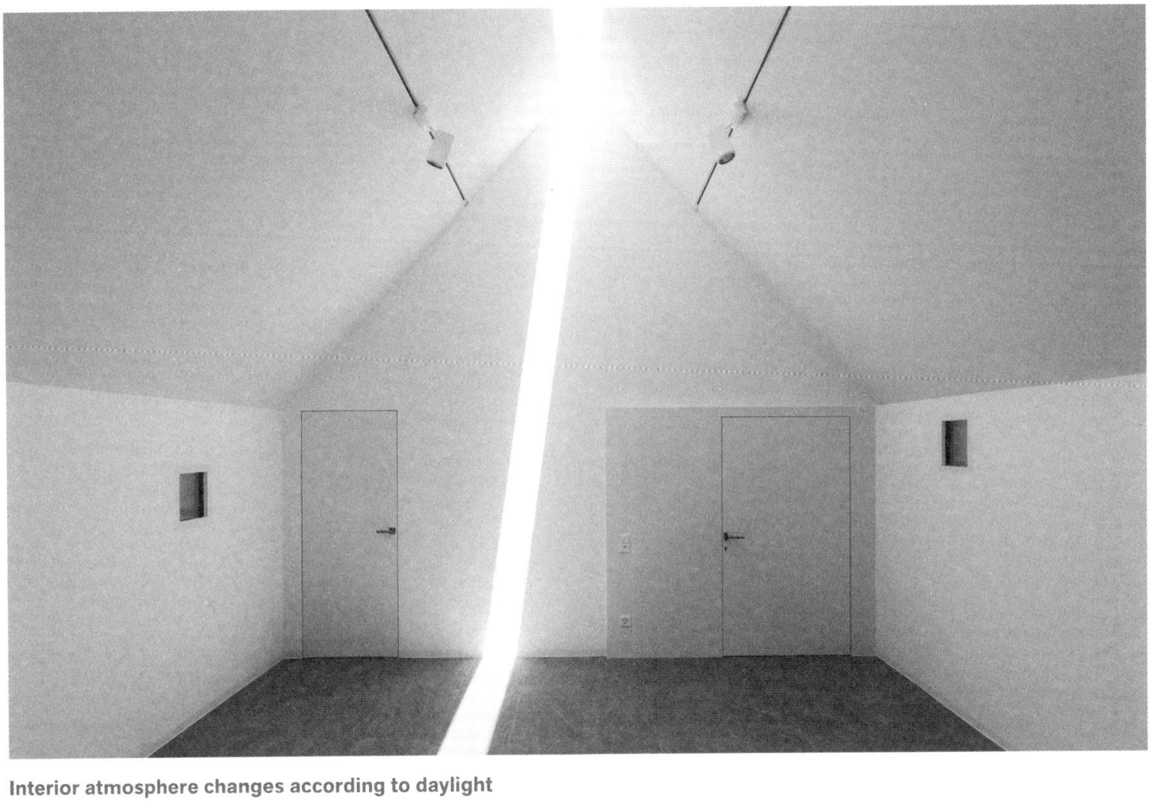

Interior atmosphere changes according to daylight

by Malik Architecture

Residence 2 at Alibaug

After construction began on the first home, the client commissioned a second with a similar program and in close proximity to the first. However, the distinct vocabulary of the first house could not be continued into the second one and a second identifiable language meant running the risk of establishing a chaotic dialogue across the site, and diluting the significance of the individual as well as the collective. The space has been planned as a variant of the C-shaped courtyard house, modified to incorporate the journey from the top of the hill to the edge of the cliff. The centrally located and tapered primary garden and pool court permeates backwards and sideways through the subterranean regions of the house, while its wide front panoramically opens onto the cliff, where a large pool overlooks a bamboo grove and the valley.

Location: Alibaug, Maharashtra, India
Architect: Malik Architecture
Year of Completion: 2013

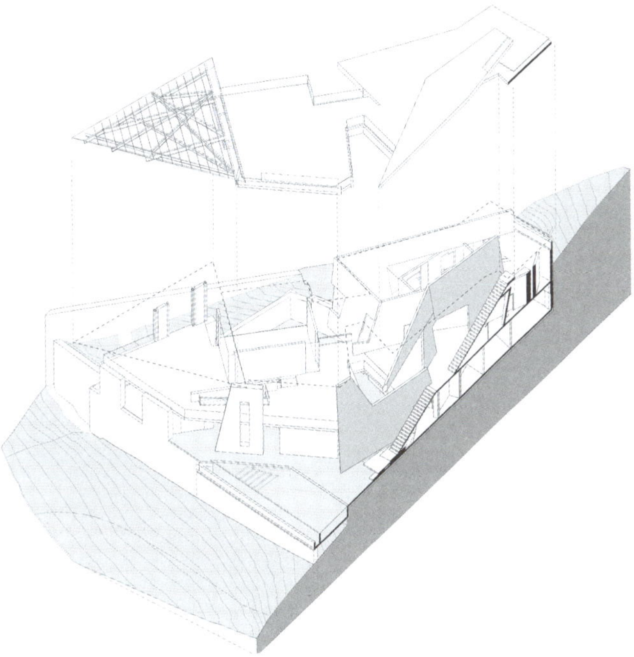

Axonometric view

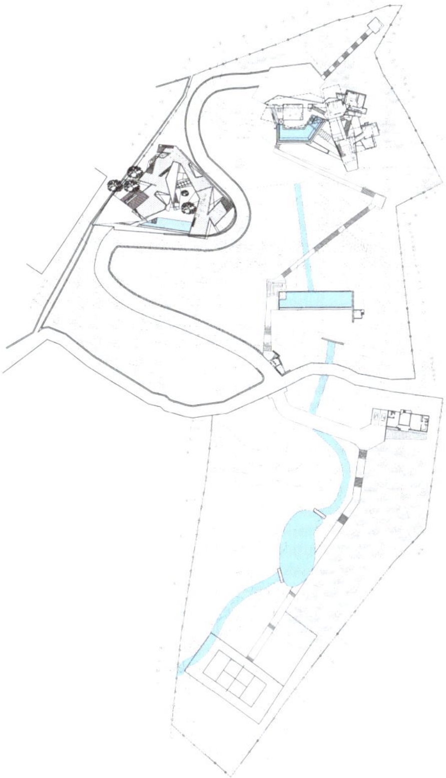

Site plan with new building on the above right

Greened roof of new home in front of first home

Gabion structure with greened roof

Windows in the gabion wall

Looking down towards pool

Pool terrace

View of landscape

by Lina Bo Bardi

SESC Pompéia

Two rough concrete blocks with several small, red-framed windows, between which run narrow offset bridges. Anyone who sees the huge building in the Palmeira workers' quarter would never guess that it houses sports facilities. Various sports fields and a swimming pool are located in the larger building, while the narrower high-rise contains the changing rooms, bars and a restaurant. Aerial walkways connect the two buildings on each level. The openings in the walls that look like the windows seen on the sports building are a particularly eye-catching feature. These can be closed from the inside using red protective grids. The brick buildings are part of the Social and Cultural Center Pompéia and once housed a former barrel factory.

Location: São Paulo, Brazil
Architect: Lina Bo Bardi
Year of Completion: 1986

Rough concrete was used for the two buildings

Aerial walkways

Cultural center in the reused old factory buildings

by Basil Spence

Coventry Cathedral

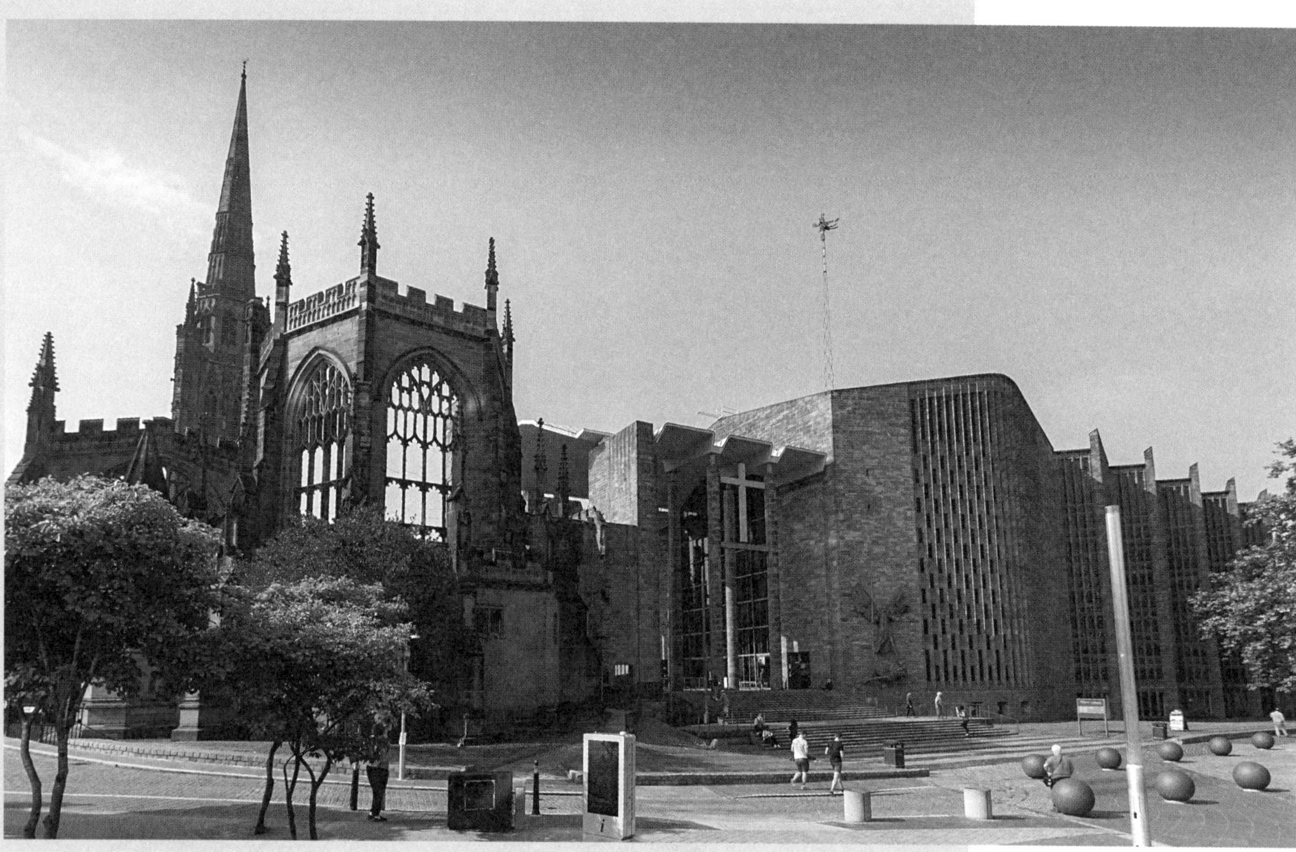

In November 1940, the cathedral and medieval city center of Coventry were almost completely destroyed by German bombs. Adjacent to the church ruins, Basil Spence built a plain brick building, structured only by narrow window slits and with a refined interior lighting design. A powerful portal construction connects the modern construction with what remains of the church ruins. The remains of the Gothic windows are still visible in the old walls, and function as a symbol of reconciliation and new beginnings. This building ensemble unites old and new, death and resurrection, darkness and light to create an impressive sense of unity.

Location: Coventry, England
Architect: Basil Spence
Year of Completion: 1962

Parts of the roofless ruins of the old cathedral next to the new building

Entrance area

CHAPTER 2

Building Images

Expressionistic
Monolithic
Formless
Upside down
Unique

According to Banham, a key aspect of brutalist buildings is that the building be presented "as a unified visual image, clear and memorable" (1966, p. 127). He saw this aspect in Hunstanton and Louis I. Kahn's Yale University Arts Center in New Haven, CT, (1951–1953), both of which are strictly orthogonal and largely flat and have very little to do with the more memorable buildings that influence our modern view of Brutalism. For us it is much more these examples that Banham describes as "...an architecture whose vehemence transcended the norms of architectural expression as violently as the paintings of Dubuffet transcended the norms of pictorial art..." (p. 68) that unite the terms Brutalism and "Imageability" (Simon Henley: *Redefining Brutalism*, p. 18). Buildings that do so are those of the tradition of Expressionism from the early 20th century. As this style was resurrected in the post-war era as Neo-Expressionism, it often overlapped with Brutalism. But not all Neo-Expressionist buildings are brutalist, and not all brutalist buildings are neo-expressionist, but in the search for a powerful, vital expression it is not uncommon for these two trends to unite.

The German Expressionists from 1910 to the 1930s were able to build only very few buildings in the years between the two world wars, but what was built anticipated the Neo-Expressionism movement, adopting for example either sharp and angular lines (Fritz Höger: Chilehaus in Hamburg, 1922–1924), or soft curving forms (Erich Mendelsohn: Einstein Tower in Potsdam, 1919–1921), that were then united with the style of Brutalism. For Nikolaus Pevsner, Expressionism was one of the most important sources of Brutalism. The fact that this highly sculptural architectural style experienced such a boom after 1945 was largely due to the technical advancements made in the field of concrete construction techniques.

Between 1911 and 1913 Max Berg proved with his Jahrhunderthalle in Breslau just how sculptural reinforced concrete could be, adding an unsupported dome over the 65-meter wide rotunda. The possibility of building such free sculptural forms was developed further in the 1930s by the engineer and architect Pier Luigi Nervi. During the 1950s he built the Palazzetto dello Sport in Rome (1956–1957), while Félix Candela designed the restaurant of the Hotel Casino de la Selva in Cuernavaca (1956). In the 1960s, Heinz Isler built the highway service area at the A1 Deitingen South in Switzerland (1968) and Ulrich Münther developed increasingly filigree buildings that explored the potential of concrete building shells. These techniques

Le Corbusier, Notre Dame du Haut, Ronchamp 1955
The Catholic church on a pre-existing pilgrimage site is one of the best-known examples of modern architecture.

Page 66: František M. Černy, Vladimir Kambersky, Emmaus Monastery, Prague, 1967
Concrete reinterpretation of the towers.

were available for both brutalist and neo-expressionist buildings, although both sought more expressive forms that moved away from technical logic of the engineers. This is clearly portrayed by Jørn Utzon's neo-expressive Sydney Opera House, built between 1959 and 1973, and not because of its technical genius, but because of the numerous building shell segments that support each other in pairs (building engineer, Ove Arup), displaying clearly visible supporting concrete beams: the striking form, rather than the refined construction, is what makes the building so expressive, even though this relied on state-of-the-art technology.

Kenzo Tange, Takamatsu Arena, 1964
The hyperbolic paraboloid covering of the hall is formed by means of cables on which are laid pre-poured concrete slabs.

Banham named Le Corbusier's later work in Ronchamp (1950–1955) and in Chandigarh (1955–1956) as examples of sculptural design. These sculptural elements – above all, the roof canopy of the Palace of Assembly in India, or the entire building volume in Ronchamp – were also defining aspects of earlier buildings, such as the roof of the Villa Savoye in Poissy and of the Unité d'Habitation. However, in Poissy the shape of the roof extension is clearly a continuation of the circular form, whereas the Unité demonstrates the free form one might expect from sculptor Le Corbusier. An important example of an enormous proto-brutalist sculptural volume is the Goetheanum in Dornach (1925–1928), an exposed concrete building commissioned by Rudolf Steiner, after his first wood anthroposophic center burnt to the ground. The giant in-situ concrete monolith, built using 15,000 cubic meters of concrete, is a solid, bulging and heavy edifice. And although it is possible to at least imagine that one can make out supports and separate building components, everything is fused together to form a three-dimensional building. This aspect of this mystical building located near Basel makes it a direct predecessor of the Notre Dame du Haut pilgrimage church, built by the Swiss architect Le Corbusier: an organic, monolithic building that largely does away with the principle of clearly separating load-bearing and non-load-bearing elements. The rounded walls, covered with shining white shot concrete, support the concrete roof of the ferroconcrete shell. There is no skeleton structure – neither of concrete as seen in the Jaoul Houses, nor of steel like in Hunstanton. And the building is in no way filigree. But this doesn't mean that Le Corbusier was not capable of producing a delicate concrete building if required, as demonstrated by the expressive form of his Phillips pavilion at the Expo 58 in Brussels. Together with the architect and Musique concrète composer Iannis

Sir Basil Spence, The Beehive New Zealand Parliament in Wellington, 1977
In the executive wing of the parliamentary complex the offices are radiated from a central core. The building is 72 meters tall. It has 10 floors above ground and four floors below.

Xenakis he designed a cluster of nine hyperbolic paraboloids of concrete slabs, the silhouette of which is similar to the swing of a conductor's baton. But in both cases – Ronchamp and the Philips Pavilion – it is the sculptural interpretation of architecture that gives the buildings their striking image.

This sculptural interpretation of architecture was particularly popular in church constructions because it enabled the architect to create much more expressive and emotional rooms than more functional styles allowed. A contributing factor to this was the Second Vatican Council (1962–1965), which recommended that new Catholic churches integrate the community more strongly into the church service – although it failed to clearly define what aspects should be reflected in the architecture of such buildings. The process of opening up the liturgy to the community had already begun in Germany in the 1920s (Johannes van Acken) and was further developed in the 1950s by Romano Guardini, the mastermind behind the Catholic youth movement Quickborn, and architect Rudolf Schwarz, who explored the idea of generating a floor plan where the altar was no longer situated in the middle, but rather in the midst of the community. The Second Vatican subsequently approved this idea, as a number of buildings using this design were already under construction when the council ended. The most important architect of such buildings was Gottfried Böhm, who continued the Expressionism begun by his father Dominikus Böhm and gave this a more modern edge by using concrete in line with Brutalism. He began to use this material to create solid, almost rock-like edifices of exposed concrete (pilgrimage church Mary Queen of Peace in Neviges, 1963–1968) or as concrete constructions with brick walls (St. Albert in Saarbrücken, 1952–1954). During the 1960s, new churches were built throughout the world – not only for the Catholic faith – where Neo-Expressionism and Brutalism come together to form a powerful synthesis. In 1961, Marcel Breuer's St. John's Abbey Church

Kenzo Tange, Olympic Arena in Tokyo, 1964
The dynamically suspended roof forms one of the most iconic building profiles in the world. The subtle curves are created by structural cables.

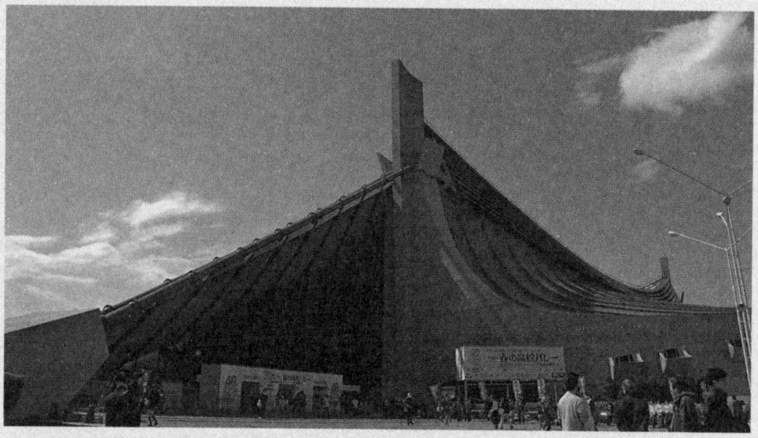

in Collegeville, MN, in 1964 Giovanni Michelucci's Chiesa di San Giovanni Battista near Florence at the A11 highway, Antonio Guacci's Church of Monte Grisa near Trieste, Eero Saarinen's North Christian Church in Columbus, IN, and Aarno Ruusuvuori's Huutoniemi Lutheran Church in Vaasa, mass and have a significant effect on the expression as a whole.

If the image of the building became too lightweight, the brutalist aspects disappear, as was the case with the folded plates seen on the United States Air Force Academy Cadet Chapel in Colorado Springs, CO: the succession of

Oscar Niemeyer, Cathedral of Brasilia, 1970
The hyperboloid structure is constructed of 16 concrete columns.

in 1965 Kenzo Tange's St. Mary's Cathedral in Tokyo, in 1966 Juliaan Lampens's Kerselare-chapel in Oudenaarde, in 1968 Claude Parent and Paul Virilio's St. Bernadette in Nevers and in 1969 Walter Maria Förderer's St. Klemenz in Bettlach, to name but a few. Sometimes the Neo-Expressionist elements are more prevalent, and sometimes the Brutalist aspects. However, they all focus on the interpretation of sculptural and emotional architectural forms using modern architectural styles that clearly present the building 17 needles of glass and aluminum, each composed of 100 tetrahedrals create the effect that the five-ton structure could be folded together. It is not heavy and sturdy like Böhms pilgrimage mountain in Neviges, where approximately 510 tons of reinforced steel are added to 7,500 cubic meters of concrete. At this towers above the parishioners one almost has the feeling that it is only faith in God that prevents the walls from burying the churchgoers. This effect can also be seen in Fritz Wotruba's Church of the

Most Holy Trinity in Vienna (1974–1976). But even in the case of the Air Force Academy Cadet Chapel, the architect sought to create an image and a memorable form, a successful tactic that has made this neo-expressionist church the most-visited man-made attraction in the state of Colorado.

In terms of image and mass in brutalist architecture, Christopher Beanland was absolutely right, when he wrote in *Concrete Concept: Brutalist Buildings Around the World* on page 14, that the bunker buildings of the Nazi architect Friedrich Tamm in the Organisation Todt could be considered to be the first brutalist buildings. His bunkers are also intended to be more than just functional, they communicate the all-important "image" of being indestructible and as solid as possible and prove themselves to be much better fortified than was necessary. Many of these concrete masses and image-building constructions are free-form structures, and attempt to avoid the classical motif of using columns and load-bearing elements as architectural details. They seek to create a more general form as a whole that has little in common with the traditional silhouettes of architectural history. Generally speaking, these are formal predecessors of BLOb architecture, which has been seeking a defining form since the 1990s that couldn't be mathematically presented using simple vectors. These Binary Large Objects and the free forms typical of Brutalism attempt to devise a form of artistic expression far removed from calculable angles and curves. However, Banham did not consider such generally free and intuitive designs for "formless (sic) buildings, such as Frederick Kiesler's 'Endless House'" (1966, p. 68) to be part of the brutalist style: for Banham, Ronchamp is initially not brutalist but "brut-Corbu" (p. 90). Even other sculptural constructions built using exposed concrete (Sydney Opera by Jørn Utzon, TWA Terminal at John F. Kennedy International Airport in New York by Eero Saarinen, 1959–1962) cannot be considered brutalist, but belong

Igor Valikievsky, Druzhba Sanatorium in Kurpaty, 1985
The Soviet sanatorium building looks like a huge planetary.

to an organic Neo-Expressionism. Accordingly, crystalline Neo-expressionism (Berlin Philharmony by Hans Scharoun, 1960–1963) is also not mentioned. In line with this definition, even buildings such as the reconstruction of the tops of the steeples at the Church of Our Lady in the Emmaus Monastery in Prague by František M. Černy and Vladimir Kambersky (1967), with their enormous intersecting concrete sails molded in a plastic casing would not be considered part of the brutalist style.

Marcel Breuer, Abbey Church of Saint John the Baptist, Collegeville, USA, 1961
Breuer's design incorporated the traditional axis of baptistery, nave, and altar in a modern concrete structure.

Banham's image is therefore much more conventional than one might expect of that era, and even in terms of Brutalism as we understand it today. The definition of a style changes over time, moving away from its original meaning as a consequence of succeeding architectural developments is fairly typical. Abbot Suger, who in 1130/35 consciously tried to build something completely new, could not envisage the effect his building in St. Denis in Paris would have on later developments. It was Giorgio Vasari who gave this style its name insulting it as "gotico", meaning barbarian. For Banham, the free forms remain something related to the building details, as demonstrated, for example, by the elements added to the roofs of Le Corbusiers Unité, or the canopy roof of Kenzo Tange's Town Hall in Kurashiki (1960). In the case of the free form designs, Banham concludes that two other elements necessary for a classification as brutalist are missing. These will be dealt with in the next chapters of this book, namely: legibility of plan and clear structure. For Banham, to be classified as brutalist, a building must remain within a relatively orthogonal grid. Jürgen Joedicke, editor of the 1966 edition of Banham's book in Germany, used the extremely sculptural Olympic buildings from Tange as an example of buildings with "image" in his article "New Brutalism: Brutalismus in der Architektur" from 1964 in the magazine *Bauen + Wohnen* (pp. 422–425).

Nowadays, the act of building an image is not only important when building churches and public buildings, but also company buildings. How strongly these buildings are influenced by the formal language of Brutalism is demonstrated by iconic buildings, such as the hermetic lightning of the Jewish Museum by Daniel Libeskind (1992–1999), the Phæno in Wolfsburg by Zaha Hadid (2000–2005) which uses gigantic free-form piloti, or buildings designed by Herzog & de Meuron, that are often extremely effective due to the use of one all-dominating material (SBB signal tower 4, Auf dem Wolf, Basel, 1992–1995).

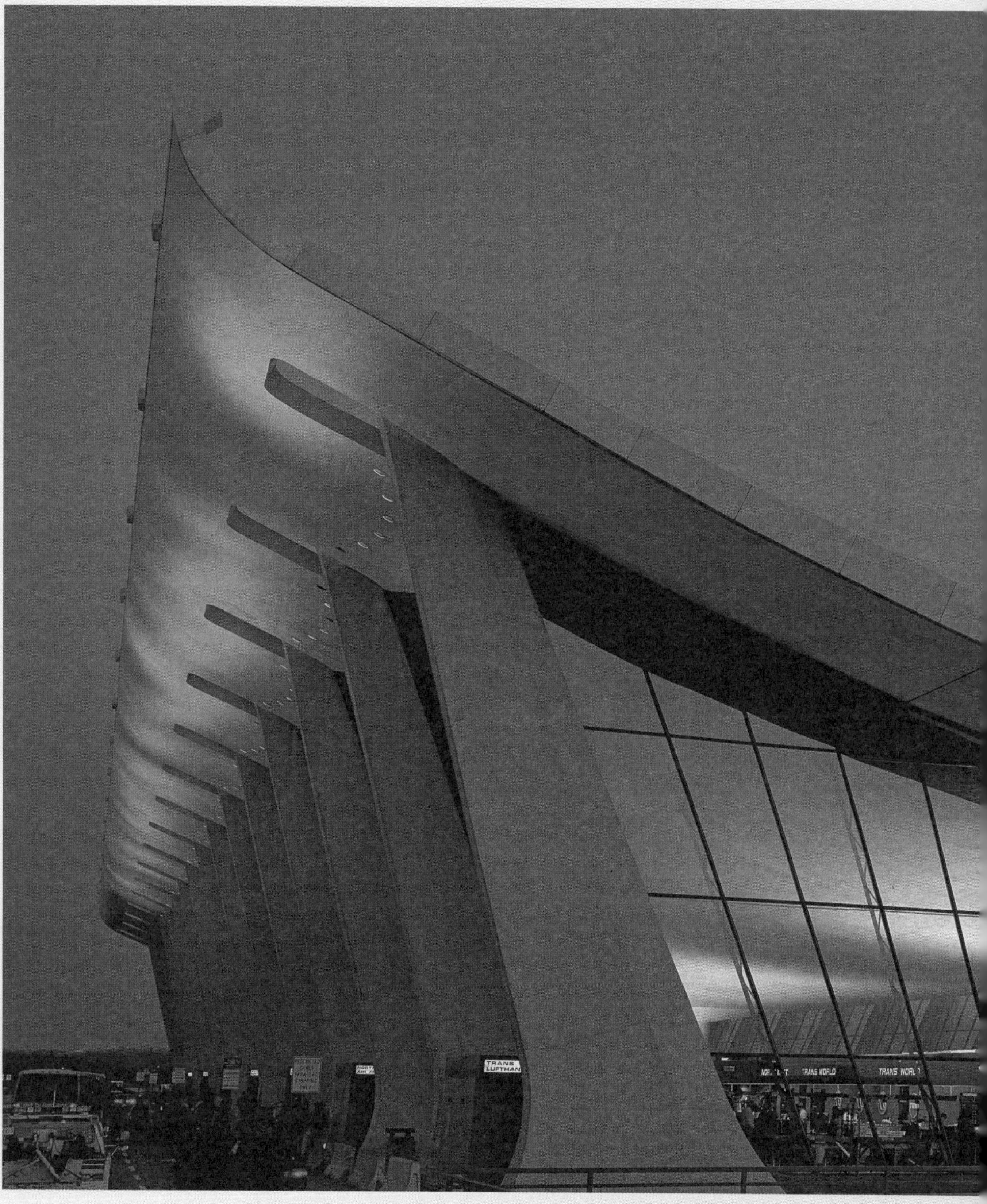
TRANS WORLD

Eero Saarinen, Dulles International Airport, Washington D.C., 1962
The roof of the terminal suspends like a hammock between two rows of columns.

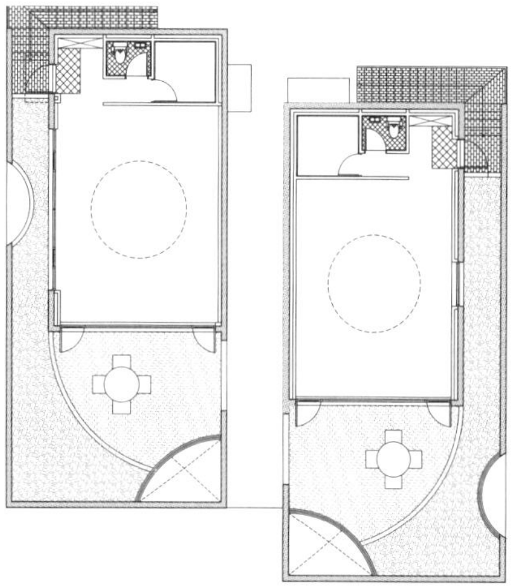

Second floor

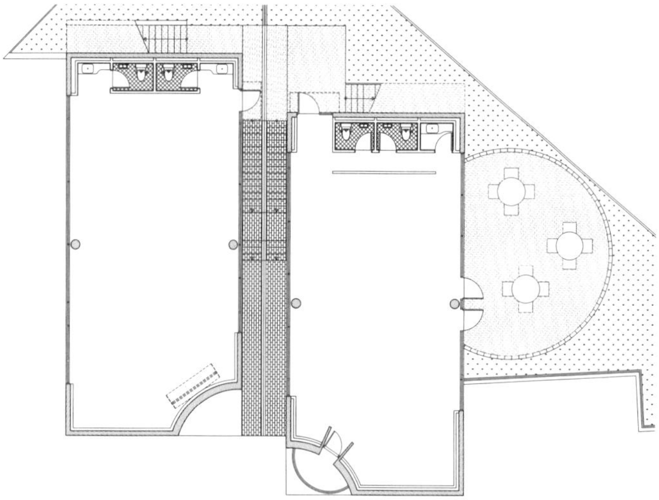

First floor

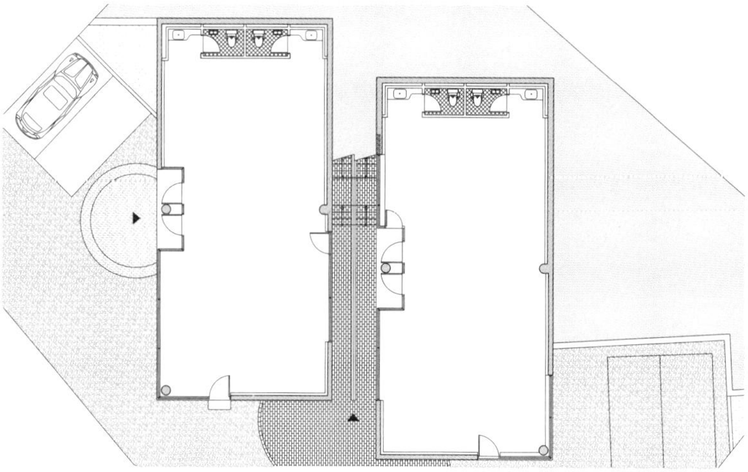

Ground floor

by Moon Hoon

Two Moon

Sometimes clients bring a clear idea or the name of a place or design as they envision it. This time a movie named Two Moon Junction surfaced as inspiration for the design when the architects first met the client. The client talked about building a cultural center arranged around a coffee shop and a gallery. A free-spirited space full of festivity but with a relaxed atmosphere. Other important criteria included providing two separate buildings; one for the client, and the other for his younger brother. The diamond-shaped site was divided into two sites accommodating two simple boxes, oriented to provide enough parking space and a passage between the two buildings. The top floors of both volumes have outdoor gardens with high walls. The two boxes interact with a large sphere with a distinct concave space that signifies a moon motif.

Location: Ilsan, South Korea
Architect: Moon Hoon
Year of Completion: 2015

Two separate buildings

Top floor balcony

Concave shapes signify moon motif

Two moon junction

View to half moon

Outdoor garden with high walls

Interior view to residential quarter

Interior view towards platform and main station

by Alex Buob

Rorschach Elevator

Rorschach's main train station is located in close proximity to the Lake Constance. An earlier quarry created the necessary space for the train station. Providing access between the residential quarter and the train station posed several difficulties. The competition required a design that would link the residential quarter with the train station, removing all possible obstacles. A pedestrian underpass is aligned axially to the station building. The new infrastructure building has been connected to this axis and continued into the residential quarter. At its foremost point, a large platform projects out over the railways and offers stunning views of the lake and surroundings. The platform has a sculptural character, the swinging opening forms a continuous band and opens towards the view.

Location: Rorschach, Switzerland
Architect: Alex Buob
Year of Completion: 2012

View from above

North elevation

West elevation

View from below

Interior view

Atrium winding upwards

Detail exterior

Exterior view

by Frank Lloyd Wright

Solomon R. Guggenheim Museum

The Solomon R. Guggenheim Museum was the last major project designed and built by Frank Lloyd Wright, opened to the public in 1959, six months after his death. This is one of his most popular projects and also took the longest to build. The exterior of the Guggenheim Museum is a stacked white cylinder of reinforced concrete that winds up towards the sky. The museum's curves are dramatic on the outside, but on the inside they have an even more striking effect. The interior is characterized by a continuous sense of flow, "one great space on a continuous floor," as Wright put it. The visitors are greeted by a vast atrium that culminates in an extensive glass dome. A continuous ramp coils up around the sides of the atrium, allowing one floor to flow seamlessly into the next. As they climb upwards, visitors experience a procession of artworks displayed along the walls.

Location: New York, NY, USA
Architect: Frank Lloyd Wright
Year of Completion: 1959

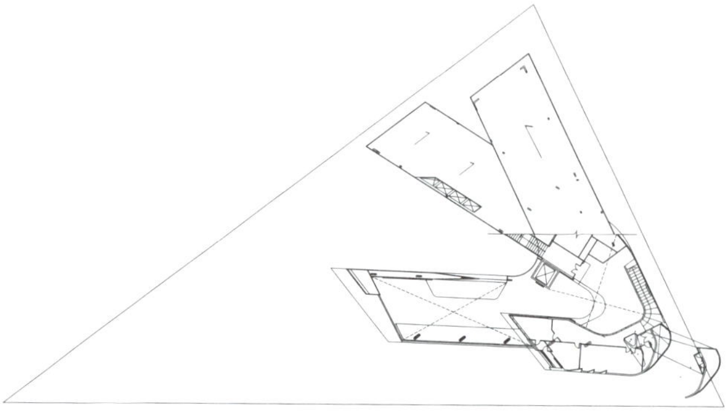

Second floor plan

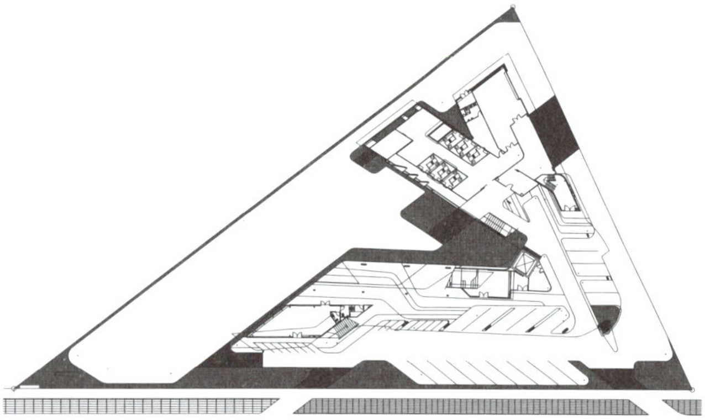

Ground floor plan

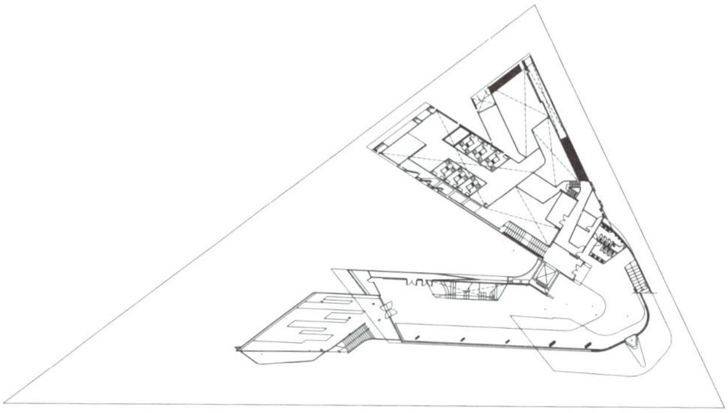

First floor plan

Dynamic volumes

by Vaslab

Honda Big Wing

This big bike center was created by architecture firm Vaslab and won an architecture competition in 2007. The architect's intention was that the construction would reinforce Honda's brand image and be a new point of interest in the city. The aesthetic form of the construction is inspired by "hugging the curve" transition; the winning moment of racing motorcycles. The two curved forms engage and compliment one another. The first curve informs the direction of the internal movement, from café and main entry through showroom, retail, education zone and warehouse. The other curve directs the path from the lounge and conference areas via offices, canteen, service center and workshop. The open space of the triangular area is hugged by these two concrete boomerangs and is reminiscent of a racing track.

Location: Praditmanutham Road, Ladprao, Bangkok, Thailand
Architect: Vaslab
Year of Completion: 2009

Heavy intersecting wings

Concrete details

Pillars inside

Slanted notches

Cantilevering block

Pillars piercing the floor slab

Church and processional route seen from the street

View of the church from processional route

by Gottfried Böhm

Mary Queen of Peace

This pilgrimage church is a towering Catholic fortress in the Protestant town of Neviges. The imposing concrete folded plate structure with its free polygonal floor plan is reminiscent of a raw, ragged and jagged rock, like an enormous tent with a number of sharp points. The wide church and procession entrance is flanked by semi-circular pilgrim houses. Inside, the church has neither a ceiling nor a vault. The roof is closed using several ridge points at a height of 34 meters and almost looks as if it has grown together all by itself, without any outside influence required. Niches, galleries, recesses, boxes and openings that look as if they have been carved into the concrete. These give one side of the building the appearance of a city cut into the rock.

Location: Neviges, Germany
Architect: Gottfried Böhm
Year of Completion: 1972

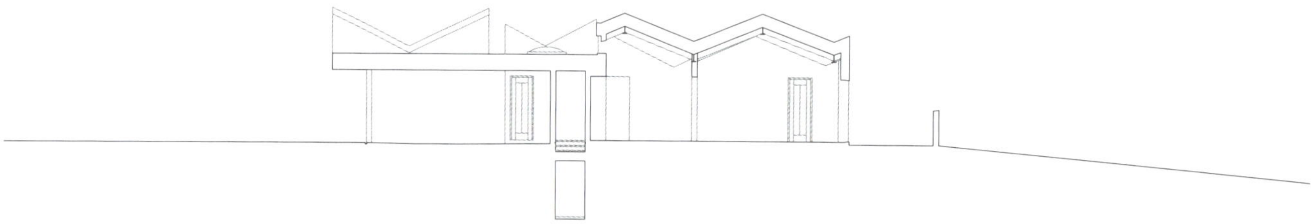

Cross section

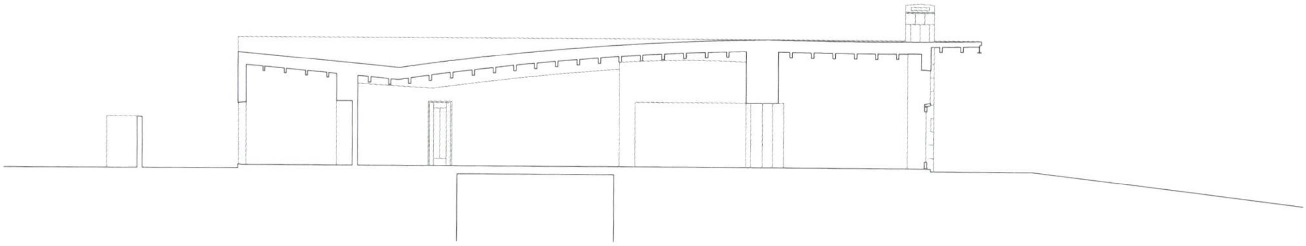

Longitudinal section

Northeast corner

by Studio Granda

B14
in Iceland

B14 is a villa on the southern periphery of a mature neighborhood. It borders a lava field and has unrestricted views of the Bláfjöll mountain ridge. Built on the site of the clients' previous house, the foundation was constructed using crushed concrete from a former dwelling located on the site. All other materials were sorted during the demolition process and recycled. The site is trapezoidal in shape; narrow on the north side and wide to the south. This simple fact was the catalyst for the folded, fan-like roof geometry that was to become so important for the development of the design. Inside, the smaller, intimate spaces, such as bedrooms, bathrooms and the laundry room, are located towards the north beneath a series of sharply pitched roofs. The living, dining and kitchen areas are housed under a gently rippling roof and have an open fireplace at each end.

Location: Capital region, Iceland
Architect: Studio Granda
Year of Completion: 2012

East garden

Bedroom wing

Basement staircase

Entrance and garage

West façade

Lower stories housing the car parks

Upper stories housing the apartments

Marina City in context

by Bertrand Goldberg

Marina City

Almost 180 meters in height, rounded towers are reminiscent of corn cobs from a distance. This Marina City residential and commercial complex on the north bank of the Chicago River is one of the most famous buildings in Chicago. Every floor beneath the 19th level has a spiral-shaped parking lot that can hold up to 896 cars. Above the 19th floor, 39 levels rise to form a city within a city. In addition to the 900 apartments, the complex also houses businesses, a theater and cinema, ice rink and bowling alley, swimming pool, restaurants and a fitness studio. All the apartments are organized radially around a central core. The layout extends like pieces of cake from the lift shaft to the outer balconies with their large semicircular form that give the towers their characteristic corn cob look.

Location: Chicago, IL, USA
Architect: Bertrand Goldberg
Year of Completion: 1968

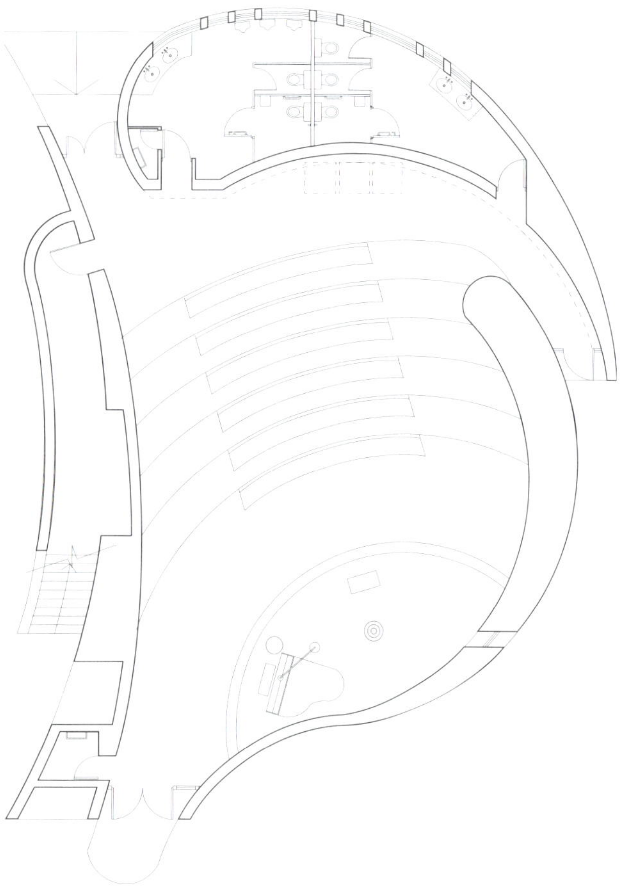

Ground floor plan

Volume is an imposing presence in the landscape

by O Studio Architects

Church of Seed

The Church of Seed is located at Luofu Mountain Scenery District – one of the seven famous Taoist Mountains in China. Although there are various kinds of Taoist and Buddhist temples in this district, western religious elements are currently underrepresented. The client intended to develop a small church to widen the spectrum of religious culture. This church provides not only worship and meditation space for Christians but also a gathering place for the locals. The design concept was triggered by the shape of a seed; a curved line follows the outline of a seed and marks the enclosing wall element. The curve is then split into three parts, and three entrances are formed. Although a seed is the starting point of this design, the church does not intend to literally illustrate this image. The abstract form of the church is conveyed through the play of light, shadow, material and texture.

Location: Luofu Mountains, Huizhou, China
Architect: O Studio Architects
Year of Completion: 2011

Site view

Curving walls

Cross-shaped incision in exterior wall

Access route

Play of light, shadow, material and texture in the interior

A long ramp leads from the driveway to the roof

The inverted dome covers the Chamber of Deputies

The two cupolas highlight the presence of the assembly chambers

by Oscar Niemeyer

National Congress of Brazil

The National Congress in Brasilia is the seat of the national government. Rising above the flat roof, two cupolas indicate the assembly chambers of Brazil's bicameral legislature: A wide white dome covers the Senate chamber, an inverted dome the Chamber of Deputies, although the concave bowl is somewhat larger than the convex dome. Both rise above the roof terrace of an elongated building, the overhang of which is supported by a row of delicate regularly spaced columns. An enormous ramp leads from the greened plaza to the roof terrace. Two slim high-rise buildings housing offices for members of parliament are located behind the horizontal construction.

Location: Brasilia, Brazil
Architect: Oscar Niemeyer
Year of Completion: 1960

Ground, first and second floor plans

Entrance

by Šépka Architekti

House in the Orchard

The proposed construction of a small family house had to be integrated into a sloping orchard full of trees. Besides the landscape, the orientation and steep slope of the plot had a significant influence in the layout of the house. The view from the living room is pointed to the valley; the other rooms are oriented to the east and south. Thanks to a skylight, the living room, situated to the north, gains light from the south. The building is designed as a wooden house set on a singular concrete pillar on the steep slope. Through the unique shape of the building, it appears as if it was dropped down from outer space. The wooden construction was designed digitally and precisely cut before assembled on site. The house is insulated with polyurethane with a top protective waterproof spray and painted gray to match the concrete.

Location: Prague, Czech Republic
Architect: Šépka Architekti
Year of Completion: 2016

View from above

Bright wooden interior

Ground floor living space

Building integrated into the sloping orchard site

Curving interior shapes

Mix of cement and stones

Church with a 70 meters mast-shaped crucifix

Entrance area

by Wojciech Pietrzyk and Jan Grabacki

The Lord's Ark Church

Nowa Huta, now a suburb of Krakow, was once a model socialist city. This was supposed to be the only town in Poland without a church. The city residents fought for years to get building permission and finally built a church building themselves, designed by Wojciech Pietrzyk. They mixed the cement with spades, and searched for the two million stones needed for the church's distinctive façade. The Lord's Ark, which is often compared with Le Corbusier's chapel in Ronchamp, has a flat elliptical floor plan. A 70-meter-tall mast in the shape of a cross towers over the church – this is a reference to Noah's Ark that settled on Mount Ararat.

Location: Krakow, Poland
Architect: Wojciech Pietrzyk and Jan Grabacki
Year of Completion: 1977

Street view

Aerial view from the Tour Montparnasse

by Marcel Breuer, Pier Luigi Nervi, Antonio Nervi, Bernard Zehrfuss

UNESCO Headquarters

The UNESCO Headquarters in Paris is a three-wing volume with a regular sequence of floor-to-ceiling windows. Supported by a series of piloti, the building has a sculptural entrance area of exposed concrete. These elements are far removed from traditional Parisian architecture, as is the separate conference building with its folded plate construction, inspired by the St. John Abbey Church in Collegeville by Breuer und Nervi (1958). American architect Marcel Breuer managed the construction, working together with the Italian master of concrete Pier Luigi Nervi and French architect Bernard Zehrfuss. Lucio Costa (Brazil), Walter Gropius (USA), Le Corbusier (France), Sven Markelius (Sweden) and Ernesto Rogers (Italy) also worked on the project in an advisory capacity.

Location: Paris, France
Architect: Marcel Breuer, Pier Luigi Nervi, Antonio Nervi, Bernard Zehrfuss
Year of Completion: 1958

IMAGE

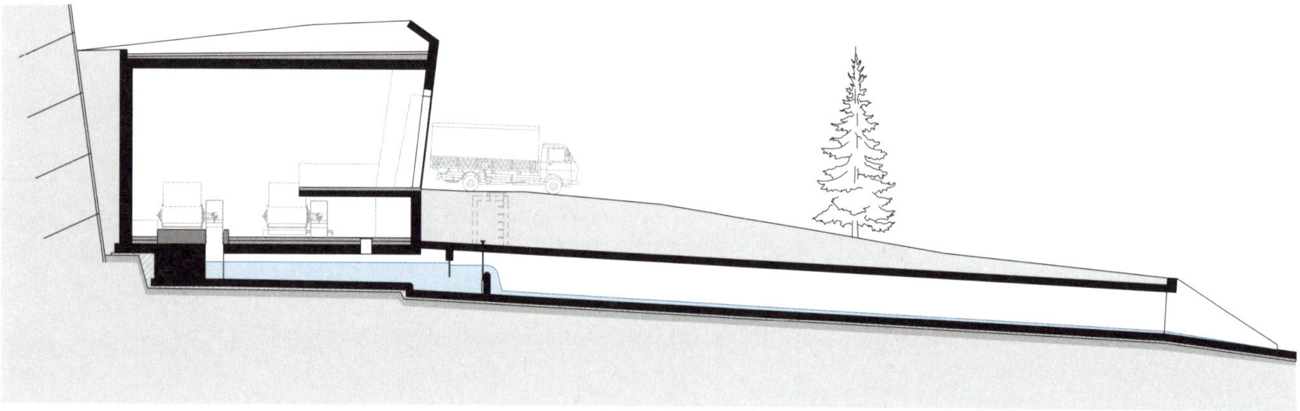

Section

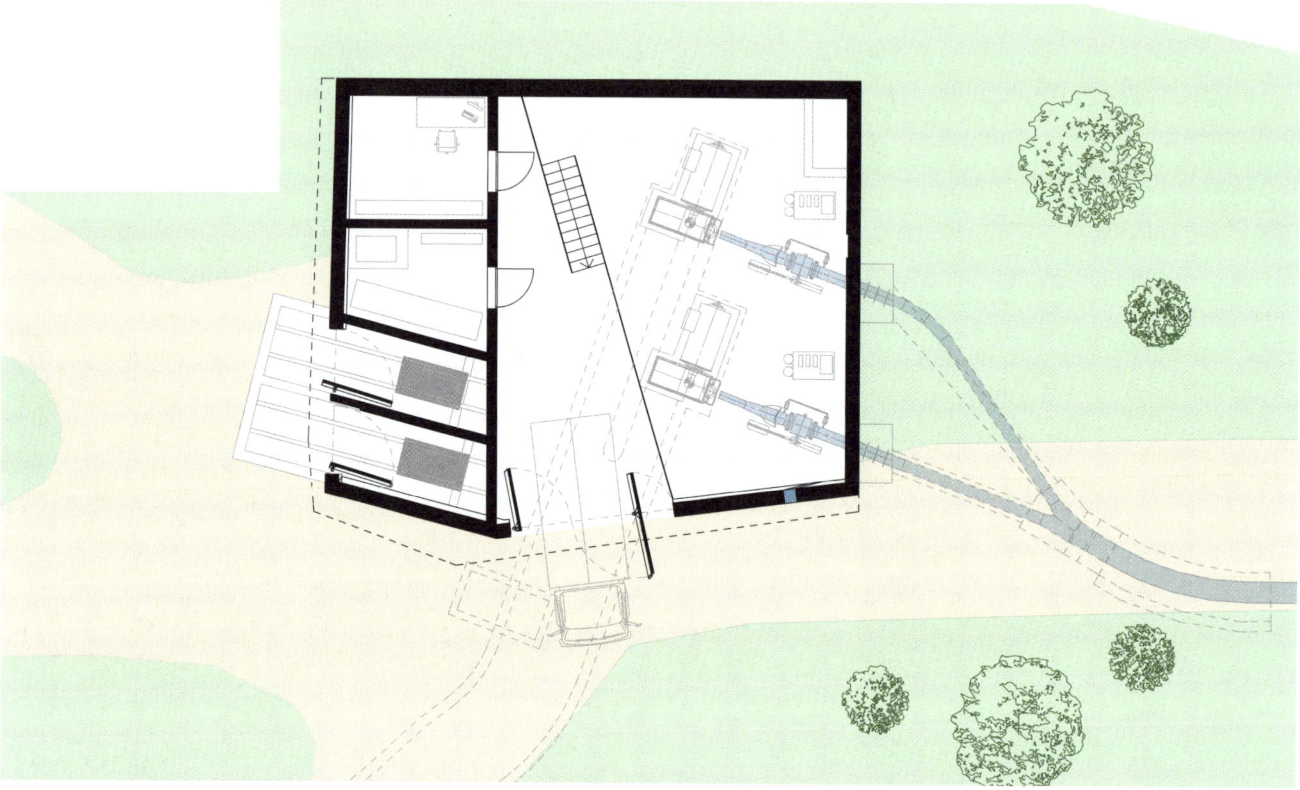

Ground floor plan

by monovolume architecture+design

Hydroelectric Power Station Winnebach

This hydraulic power station is located in Vintl in the village of Dörfl. Due to the limited amount of space available, the powerhouse has been built partially into the slope. The design comprises a simple building that has been carefully adapted to suit the landscape and local characteristics. The new powerhouse is intended to look like a large rock, jutting out of the sloping site. As well as incorporating various angles, edges and sloping faces, the powerhouse concept is reinforced by the use of just a few main materials, including concrete, steel and glass. This similarity reinforces the "natural" appearance and helps the building blend into its surroundings. The similarity to a rock is emphasized by the "veins" that cut through it. These veins are formed of glass bands and run across the building allowing views into the machine hall in some areas.

Location: Vintl, Dörfl, Italy
Architect: monovolume architecture+design
Year of Completion: 2009

Building looks like a rock jutting from the hillside

Glass bands embedded in wall

Corner detail

Light shining through glass bands at night

Interior and machinery

Building in context

Concrete structure clad in Portland stone

Concrete trusses held together by ring beams

by Frederick Gibberd

Liverpool Metro-politan Cathedral

The now listed building was the final of many proposed designs for a cathedral in Liverpool and was built between 1962 and 1967, mainly out of concrete with Portland stone cladding and an aluminum roof covering. 16 boomerang-shaped concrete trusses, held together by two ring beams, support the main building, with the bell tower, a wedged-shaped structure, at the entrance. Due to its shape, it is often compared to Oscar Niemeyer's cathedral in Brasilia. The rapid and economical construction of the cathedral led to many flaws in the building, mainly a leak in the aluminum roof, which was repaired in the 1990s. Several of the original materials where thereby replaced by more robust elements such as glass-rein-forced plastic instead of the mosaic tiles and stainless steel in the lantern instead of aluminum.

Location: Liverpool, England
Architect: Frederick Gibberd
Year of Completion: 1967

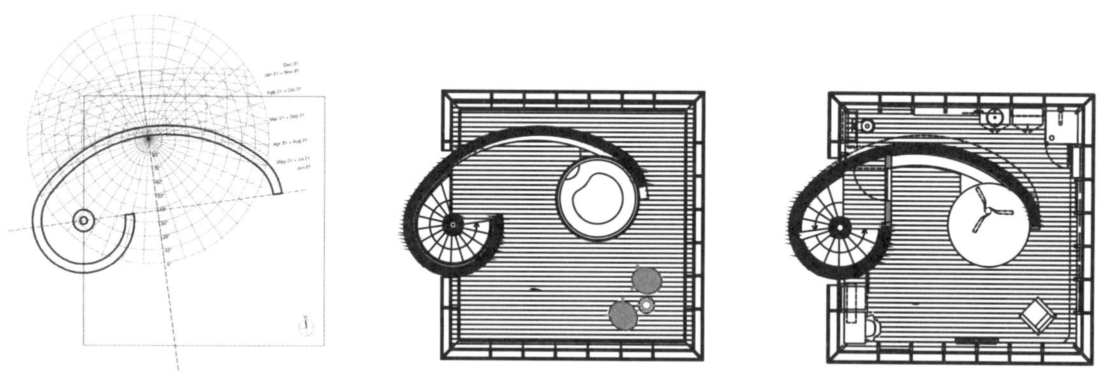

Sun path diagram, solarium roof plan, master bedroom

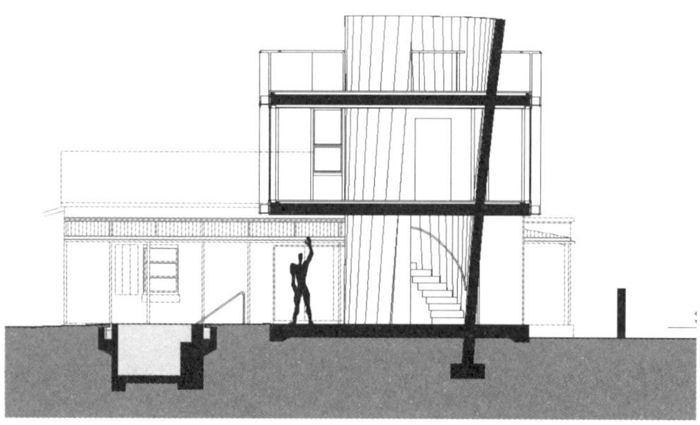

Section

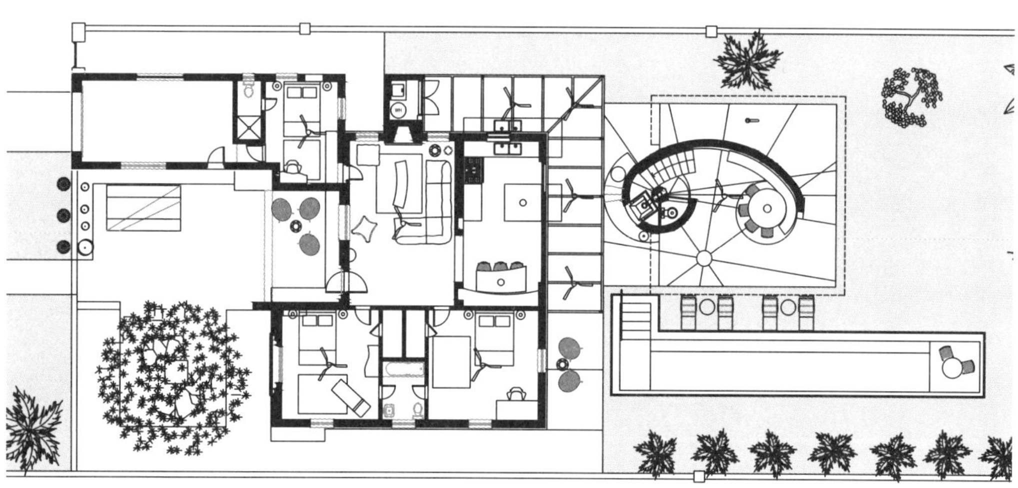

Ground floor plan

by Studio Christian Wassmann

Sun Path House

The Sun Path House is a concrete structure adjacent to a 1930s bungalow. The sun path diagram inspired its shape and the sun becomes a central feature of the design, fostering the vitality and health of the inhabitants. This project is a three-story extension with a large kitchen that serves to connect the new extension to the existing house. An upwardly spiraling wall is located behind the bungalow: this is simultaneously structural, functional and sculptural, serving as the spine of the project. The heart of the Sun Path House is a solarium positioned at the top of the house. The curved wall at its precipice maps the path of the sun on the summer's solstice. During this passage, the sun's rays are reflected from the wall onto the deck. The form of the Sun Path House is a result of a dialogue with the original house and the cosmos.

Location: Miami Beach, FL, USA
Architect: Studio Christian Wassmann
Year of Completion: 2015

View through solarium from below

Interior

Colorful illumination

View from the garden

Partially greened exterior

Extensive views through large windows

Curved solarium wall

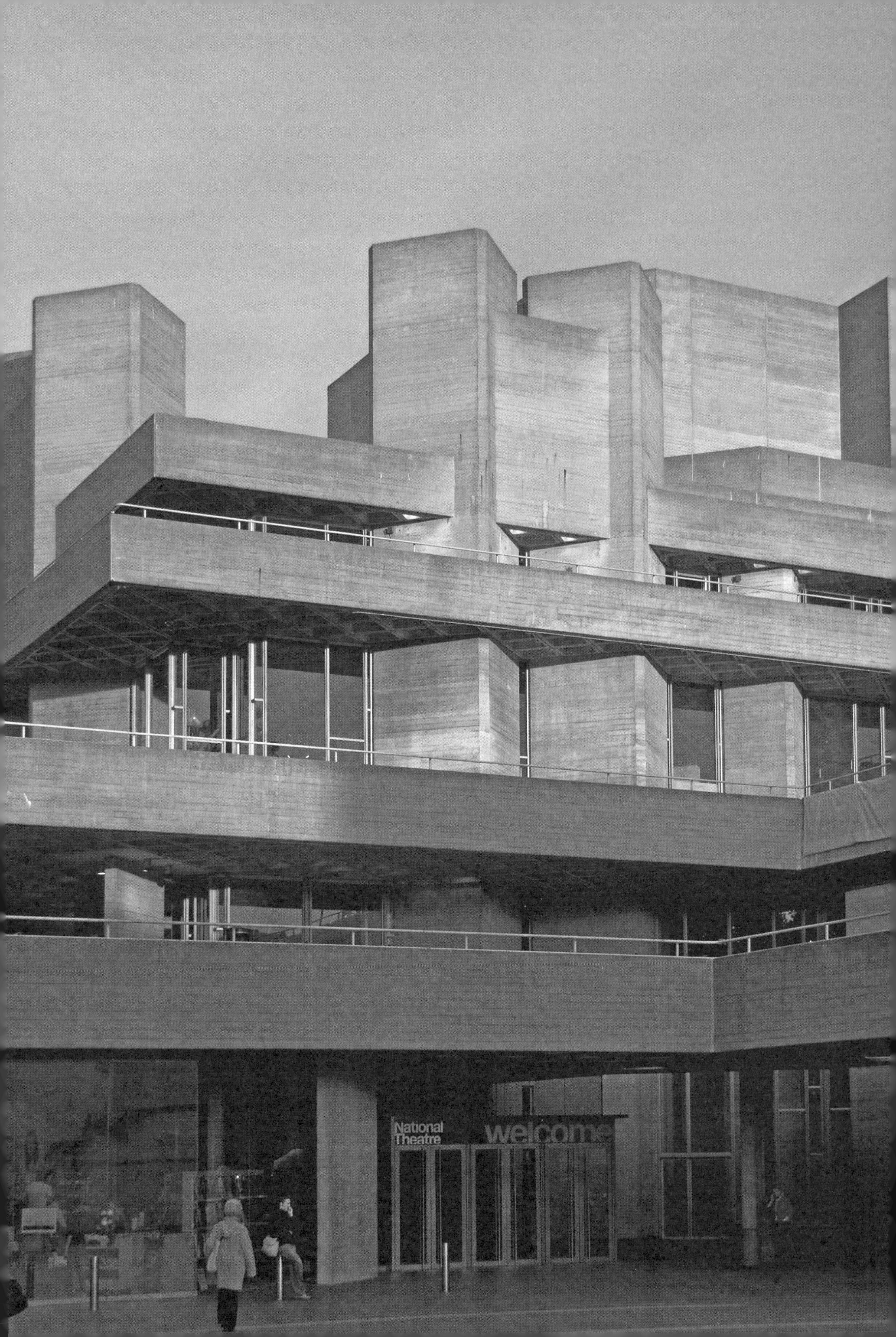
National
Theatre
welcome

CHAPTER 3

Legibility of Plan

Terraces
Cantilevers
Setbacks
Stacking
Upside down

In order for a building to classify as brutalist, Banham also demands a "legibility of plan". Both of his examples are extremely legible: the Smithson's school building and Louis I. Kahn's Yale University Art Gallery in New Haven, CT, 1951–1953. Both of these have a clearly structured façade – metal structuring in Hunstanton and concrete in New Haven – with large-scale brick walls, repeated glass elements and legible orthogonal volumes. As Banham writes of Kahn's building, on page 44, "Like Hunstanton, it has a formal and axial plan (rather more sophistic in its planning, too) and its basic aesthetics lean heavily on the frank expression of structure and material." (1966, p. 44). The formal and axial plan make the spatial arrangement visible even from the outside, adhering to Banham's idea of "warehouse aesthetics" – even though the Yale University Art Gallery hides a few surprises inside in terms of spatial formulation.

Generally speaking, the geometric orthogonal legibility is directly inspired by the Classical Modern and the Brick Functionalism of the 1930s. This also applies when one stands inside Kahn's building, and to the exposed concrete rotunda – one of the surprises – that is easily legible as a simple geometric tube based on a round floor plan. As a radical formulation, this is, like Konstantin Melnikov's round house in Moscow (1926–1929), an extremely important aspect of image creation. Further examples, where legible basic forms are fused together to create a characteristic image, are Frank Lloyd Wright's Solomon R. Guggenheim Museum in New York, 1956–1959, or Oskar Niemeyer's National Congress in Brasilia, 1958–1960, where – typical of its era – the image-creating elements come together on a podium-like base, which itself is located on a recessed ground floor and almost appears to float in the air. However, this is based on simple geometric forms and volume arrangement and is just one possible way of configuring the building volumes that today characterize Brutalism, but it is not the most common.

A more complex design is much more typical than the use of interlocking boxes and singular tubes: Instead of simply positioning

Paul Rudolph, Yale University Art Gallery in New Haven, 1963
The building is one of the earliest known examples of Brutalist architecture in America.

Page 124: Denys Lasdun, Royal National Theatre, London, 1976

various forms next to each other, these are often stacked one above the other. This is typical of numerous staggered terrace apartment blocks. The terraced houses at Denys Lasdun's New Court at the University of Cambridge's Christ's College (1966–1970) also demonstrate a legible structure, while

gmp Architekten von Gerkan, Marg und Partner, Airport Tegel, 1974
On the outer façades there is a strong contrast with the gray concrete, the bronze hues of the window glazing and smooth façade surfaces.

Habitat 67 by Moshe Safdie in Montréal is a wild staggering of staggered and stacked volumes, cantilevered sections and interlocking exposed concrete cubes of 5 × 11 × 3 meter elements spread across 12 floors. Single apartments are divided between up to four stories and the useable area varies from 54 to 153 square meters – with no trace of legibility. The desired complex arrangement with communal spaces between the unites and neighborhoods, will be investigated in chapter five, which will look at the points of contact with Team Ten, Structuralism and Metabolism.

There are also numerous examples of public buildings where Brutalism refrains from pursuing simple legibility, and expresses instead complex staggered forms. A typical example of this is the Royal National Theatre in London. This is a truly brilliant design for a number of reasons. It was built by Denys Lasdun between 1951 and 1976. Numerous staggered levels, partially interlocking volumes, complex access routes, bridges, rounded and cantilevered stairways, randomly positioned cubes all make this building rather illegible, at least at first glance.
The use of numerous cantilevered elements are a typical Brutalism motif, particularly in residential buildings. These give the building a more horizontal appearance and emphasize the individual stories as independent building plates. The structural skeleton upon which the building is based does not show the typical balanced relationship between supporting and loaded sections, rather favoring the expression of load.

Lasdun's use of form is not without precursors. The horizontal emphasis, one of the fundamental characteristics of the Classical Modern style (bands of windows), the "unnecessary" cantilevering of apparently heavy (but not independent) volumes can be seen on Alvar Aalto's Town Hall in Säynätsalo, 1949–1952. The staggered volumes can be seen in earlier cultural buildings such as the theater in Münster, built by Harald Deilmann, Max Clemens von Hausen, Ortwin Rave and Werner Ruhnau between 1954 and 1956. The National Theatre

Walter Maria Förderer, Chur Konvict, 1969
Three elongated, flat-roofed buildings from exposed concrete pile up to form a stepped structure with a total of nine levels.

Denys Lasdun, New Court of Christ's College in Cambridge, England, 1970
The brutalist built in ziggurat form is called the "Typewriter".

might be illegible, but a further group of brutalist buildings do display a certain legibility – but not in the way Banham meant; he supported a much more sensible and sober design. The practice of testing the boundaries of statics to their extreme is demonstrated by the cantilevering balconies and the building volumes themselves that were increasingly characterized by wildly cantilevered sections. The Birmingham Central Library by John H. Madin (1969–1974) was torn down in 2016, but was a prime example of where the heavy concrete stories were not only arranged above a largely glazed lower level, but where the upper levels were also larger and more prominent than the lower levels. Buttresses are positioned in front of the glazed lower story. They do fulfill a static necessity but do emphasize the absurdity of the arrangement as well. While it might be possible to trace this reversed structure back to Le Corbusier's piloti, in terms of Brutalism, this is taken to a new extreme form of Mannerism, similar to the upside-down pyramids seen in the aforementioned Slovak Radio Building.

In addition to the horizontal staggering, vertical staggering was also sometimes implemented, a technique that can also reduce legibility. This becomes particularly clear on the Yale Art & Architecture Building in New Haven, CT, by Paul Rudolph, who was arguably the most important American Brutalist aside from the non-native Marcel Breuer, and was awarded the commission during his six-year stint as departmental chair, between 1958 and 1965. The building was completed in 1963 and had a complex floor plan comprising 37 terraced levels spaced across seven main stories and two base-

Van den Broek and Bakema, Town Hall Terneuzen, 1973
The layout of the bold and sculptural concrete building is like an upward going spiral.

ment floors. The exterior is dominated by the closed, tower-like sections that project out from the actual building volume. For Nikolaus Pevsner, who delivered the inauguration speech in 1963, the building wasn't particularly functional, neither in terms of its composition nor its floor plan and surface treatment – with smooth exposed concrete sections and with bush-hammered areas. As a whole, it boasted a rather conglomerate appearance, more so than most building dominated by vertical staggered elements.

To what extent this entire group of sculptural free-formed buildings were sound and legible in a Bauhaus view remains open – some certainly to a great extent, such as the numerous sports halls like Alexander Buchanan Campbell's Dollan Aqua Centre in East Kilbride, 1965, or Kenzo Tange's Olympic buildings in Tokio, 1961–1964. Banham did acknowledge the latter, claiming that Tange featured largely in the history of Brutalism with buildings like the brutalist Kurashiki City Hall (1957–1959).

However, more prevalent than any of these mass divisions, and more common even than the horizontal staggering, is the balanced orthogonal building volume, where the walls are structured within the basic form of the building. The Unités by Le Corbusier are the most famous examples of this, with their flat façades studded with windows and balconies arranged to form patterns. The issue of how the walls are structured is the subject of the next chapter.

John H. Madin, Birmingham Central Library, 1974
The concrete building with its bold geometry, inverted ziggurat sculptural form and monumental scale is an icon of British Brutalism.

SPEED
LIMIT
25

Belt, Lemon and Lo with John Carl Warnecke and Associates, Hawaii State Capitol, Honolulu, 1969
Northeast and southeast elevations.

by kister scheithauer gross architekten und stadtplaner (ksg)

Maria-Magdalena Church

This unusual church building is located at the heart of the new Rieselfeld city quarter. Two churches, Protestant and Catholic, are united in one building and combined to form an ecumenical religious space. The two main walls are folded several times as they progress across the space, sloping gently outwards and inwards at irregular intervals. This gives the impression of openness and flexibility. True to traditional church constructions, this church also has a nave and two side aisles. A large ecumenical space is created when the floor-to-ceiling walls are opened. All the exterior and interior walls, including the moveable dividing partitions, have been built using high-quality exposed concrete. A striking timber beam ceiling fills the space between the powerful walls and draws the nave and two side aisles all under one roof.

Location: Freiburg, Germany
Architect: kister scheithauer gross architekten und stadtplaner (ksg)
Year of Completion: 2004

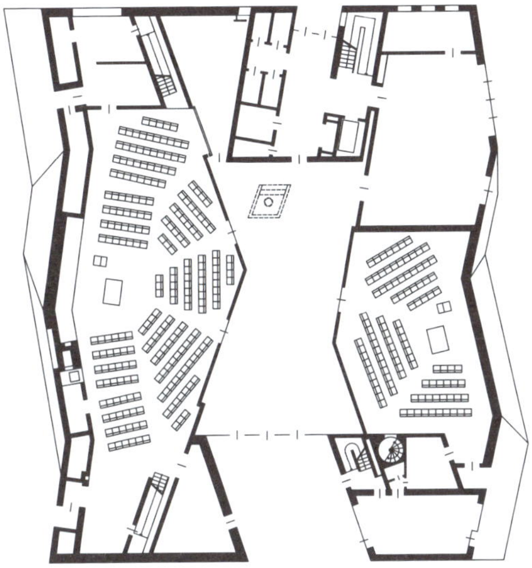

Ground floor plan: two churches configuration

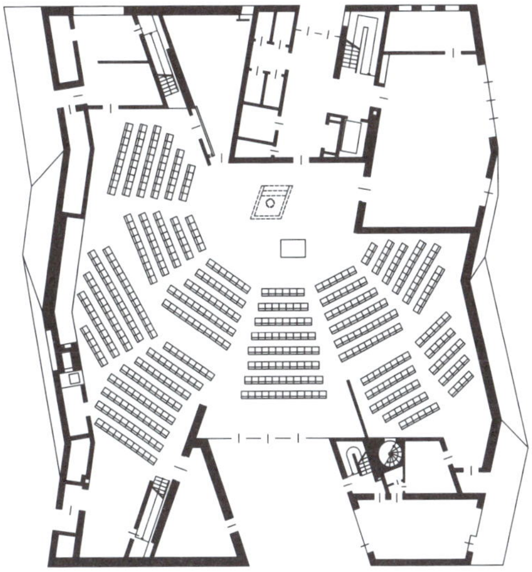

Ground floor plan: one church configuration

Protestant and Catholic church with the connecting central hall

Entrance courtyard and accordion partition with large window of Protestant church space

View from Catholic to Protestant church

The baptismal font

Folded exterior wall of Catholic church space

Lighting in Catholic church space

by Moshe Safdie

Habitat 67

Habitat 67 was designed by the Israeli-Canadian architect Moshe Safdie and functioned as the Canadian Pavilion for the World Exposition in 1967. The project originated as Safdie's Bachelor thesis, entitled "A Case for City Living." Safdie later developed this into a complete master plan which contained shopping centers, a school, and 1,000 housing units. The scheme was accepted, but later reduced to only 158 residential units. The on-site prefabrication system should have reduced the cost of production, but due to the reduction of the project's mass scale, costs were much higher than expected. The project was constructed from 354 completely prefabricated modules, stacked in various combinations and connected by steel cables. Each apartment is accessed via a series of pedestrian streets and bridges.

Location: Montréal, Canada
Architect: Moshe Safdie
Year of Completion: 1967

View from Montréal's port

View from street level

by Vector Architects

Seashore Library

Located approximately three hours drive from Beijing, this library is positioned inside a vacation compound along Bohai Bay. While Beijing has been experiencing massive economic growth and urban development, many people are critical of the drop in the standard of living. This vacation compound aims to create a quality-living area closer to nature. The design of the library focuses on exploring the symbiotic relationship between the space, movement of visitors, the shifting light ambience, ventilation and the ocean view. During spring, summer and fall, it not only serves the community residents, but is also open to the public. The library houses a reading area, a meditation space, activity room, a bar and a resting area. The architects have established a distinctive relationship between space and the ocean, defining how light and air enters each room.

Location: Beidaihe New District, Heibei, China
Architect: Vector Architects
Year of Completion: 2015

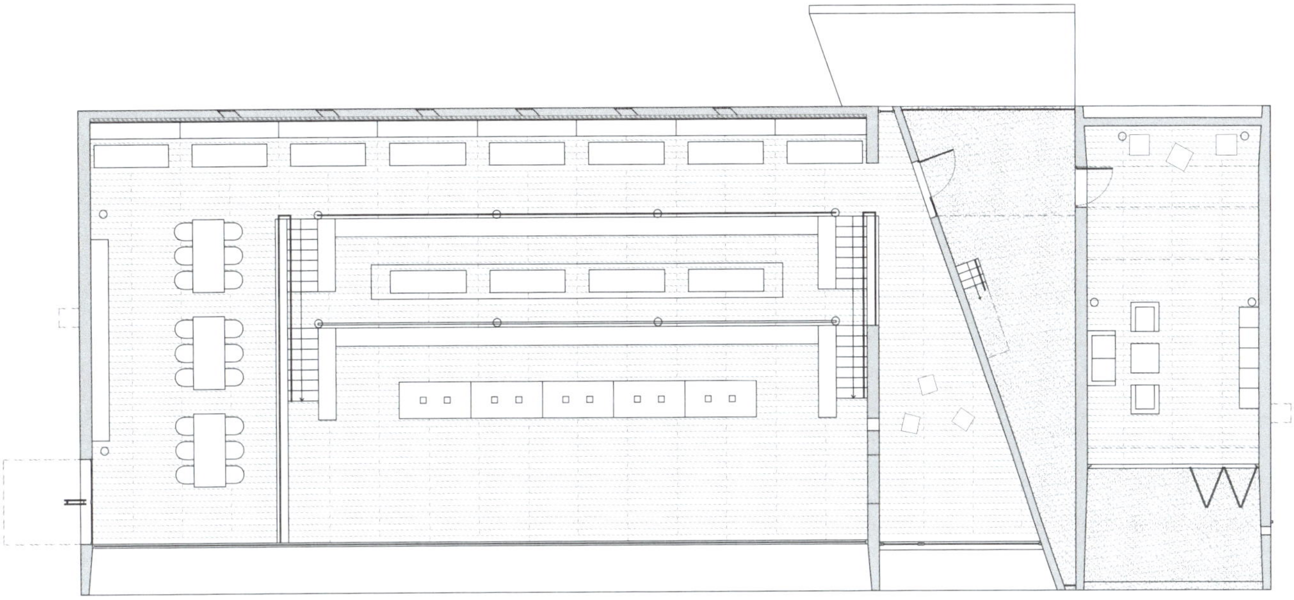

Second floor plan

Ocean view

Slim openings instill a sense of dynamism

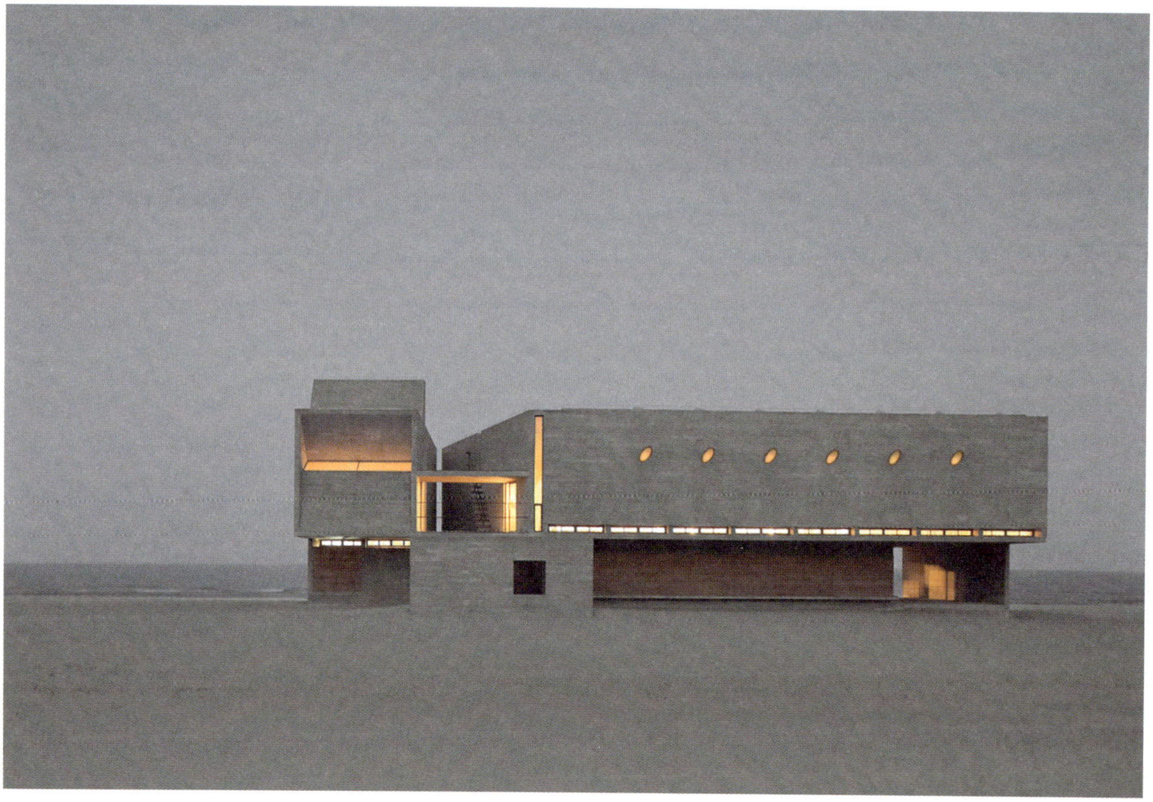
Building at night

The solid concrete structure emits a sense of calm and quiet

Series of voids and walls

Stunning views of the ocean

by Colomer-Aceves Arquitectes

Horta Vermella Nursery School

This school building is located between two different neighborhoods, trying to connect them. The school's boundaries have been closed in to enable the creation of the largest playground possible, separated from the main road. The building is built of concrete using timber formwork, and has been painted black to create a contrast between the walls and the windows. The lightness of the interior contrasts the dense and sturdy exterior. Sculptural elements characterize both the interior and exterior. Folded concrete walls rise on the outside, creating a series of surprising spaces and protective overhangs. Inside, the vertical space reminds one of the forest that used to be there, and the spiraling staircases and large windows add to the sculptural character, giving the building a more lightweight and less oppressive esthetic.

Location: Vic, Barcelona, Spain
Architect: Colomer-Aceves Arquitectes
Year of Completion: 2008

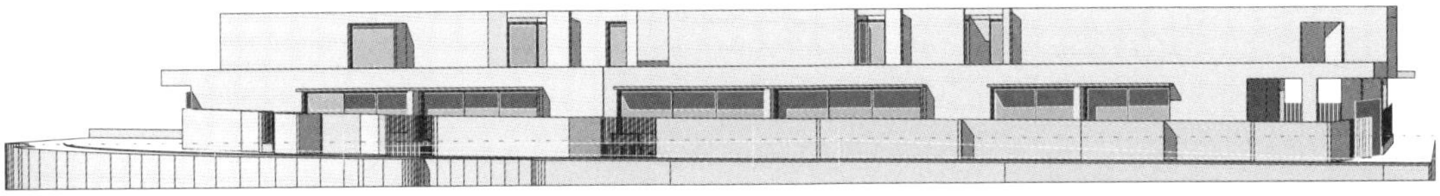

Street elevation

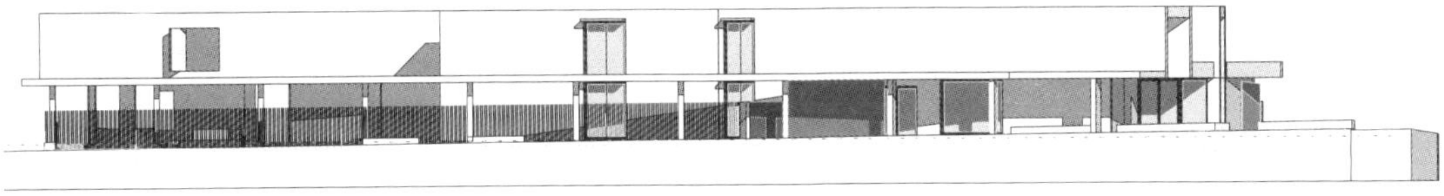

Car park elevation

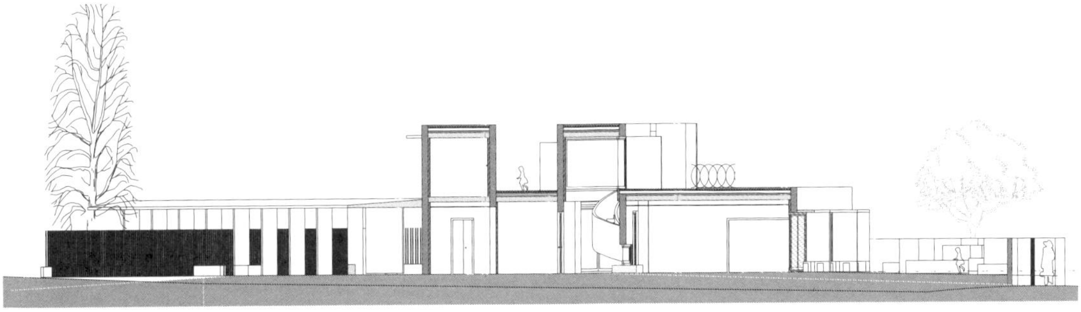

Section

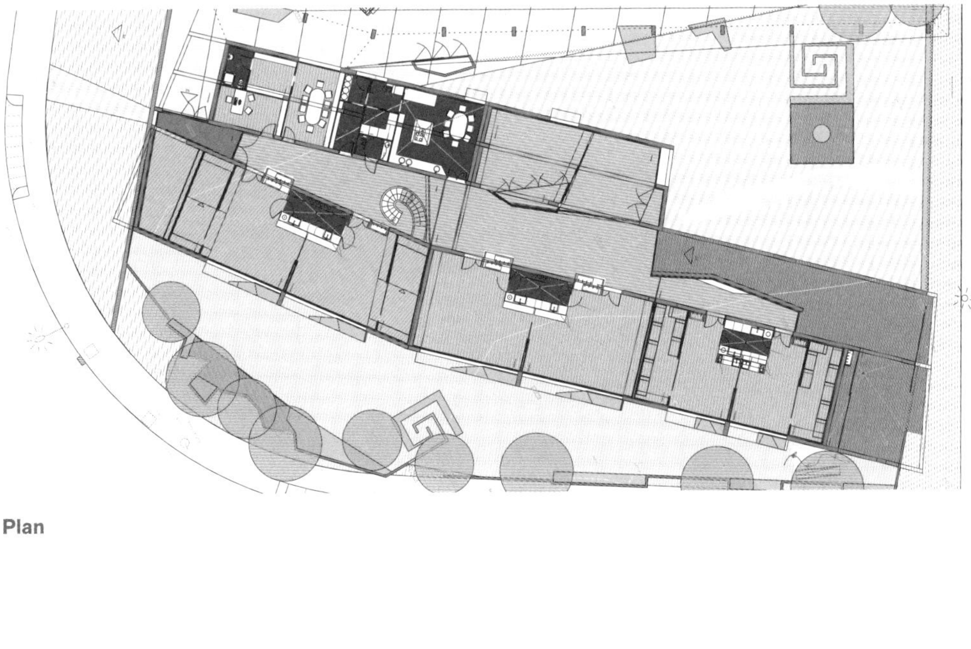

Plan

Folded concrete walls

Interior in light colors

Exterior façade painted black

Large windows add to the sculptural character

by Louis I. Kahn

Salk Institute for Biological Studies

This independent, non-profit, scientific research institute was founded by Jonas Salk in 1960. He developed the polio vaccination and wanted to build a research facility where people would be able to work towards helping others. Together with the architect Louis I. Kahn, he designed a campus that would serve as an ideal research and working environment. Two buildings are grouped around a central courtyard with a watercourse running through the middle. Both buildings are built entirely of exposed concrete and have windows. Window fronts and shutters are all made of untreated mahogany wood. The building is almost church-like in appearance and offers views of the Pacific Ocean, functioning as a meeting point for researchers who wish to exchange information about current projects and advancements.

Location: La Jolla, CA, USA
Architect: Louis I. Kahn
Year of Completion: 1965

View from the back of the building

Interior courtyard with fountain

Side view

by Nieberg Architect atelieraxelnieberg

Braunschweig Residence

The entrance area is arranged to form an exterior and an interior zone. The atrium is visible from the outside via a clearly defined slit that is also marked by a concrete access route. The ground floor is organized as a classical living area, while the flowing spatial sequence allows close contact with the exterior areas. The windows wrap around the corners of the building and provide interesting views of and through the interior rooms. An exposed concrete stair flanked by dynamic lighting leads to the upper floor where the bedrooms and bathrooms for the entire family are located. The gallery is home to a large and imposing desk that also functions as an additional workspace for the children. The upper floor is surrounded by a loggia that also functions to shade the building from the sun.

Location: Braunschweig, Germany
Architect: Nieberg Architect atelieraxelnieberg
Year of Completion: 2013

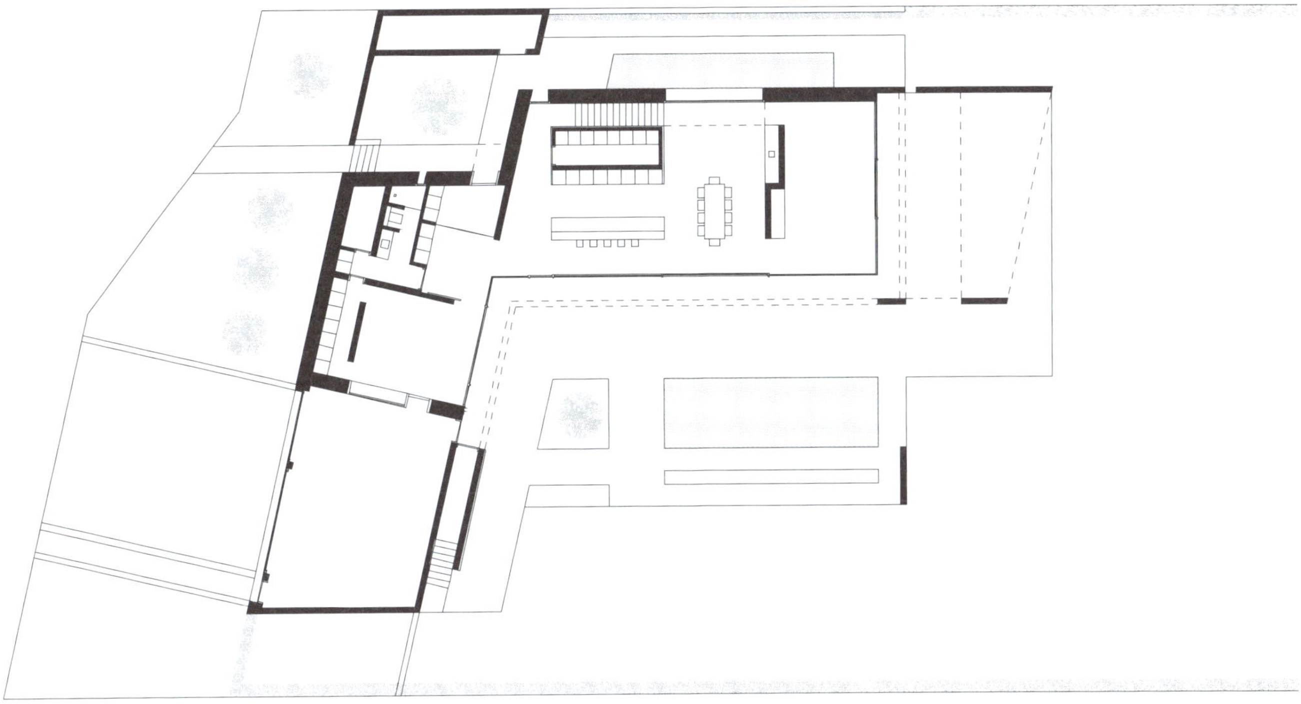

Ground floor plan

Front view

Terrace

Stairs to roof terrace

Loggia

Gallery

Fireplace

by Edmond Lay, Pierre Layré-Cassou and Pierre Dugravier

Caisse d'Epargne Mériadeck

These round slabs have been stacked on top of one another, with thin window bands between: the former Caisse d'Épargne in Meriadeck, a modern city quarter in Bordeaux, shares some similarities in terms of its shape to Frank Lloyd Wright's Guggenheim Museum in New York. But while that building has a shining white façade, and a relatively lightweight appearance, the French building appears heavy and solid. Brown-yellow exposed aggregate concrete with rough aggregate characterizes the appearance of the building and lends it an almost organic opulence. This is not without reason; when the building was built, exposed aggregate concrete was perceived as a natural material. Typical aggregates were river pebbles, washed from the earth by the river and then polished until they were round.

Location: Bordeaux, France
Architect: Edmond Lay, Pierre Layré-Cassou, Pierre Dugravier
Year of Completion: 1974

Horizontal composition

Detail of concrete

Street view

by Bunker Arquitectura

Sunset Chapel

This chapel has been built at the summit of a hill that overlooks the bay of Acapulco, an area famous for its beautiful sunsets. The client brief was simple: The chapel had to make the most of the spectacular views, and the sun had to set exactly behind the altar cross – of course, this is only possible twice a year during the equinoxes. Two elements obstructed the views; large trees and abundant vegetation, and a behemoth boulder blocking the main sight of the sunset. In order to clear these obstructions, the chapel had to be raised at least five meters. Acapulco's hills are made up of huge granite rocks lying on top of each other, so the architects attempted to make the chapel look like just another colossal rock lying on the cusp of this pile of boulders.

Location: Acapulco, Mexico
Architect: Bunker Arquitectura
Year of Completion: 2011

Raised view

View at night

Chapel surrounded by abundant vegetation

View at sunset

View at night

Chapel interior

Chapel representing a granite rock

by Atelier BNK

Numata Elementary School

This small school has just one class in each grade. Numata lies in a region of heavy snowfall, and because it is closed in by snow for the majority of the year, the aim of this project was to create a school that provides a compact yet diverse space focused on indoor activities for children. Excluding the south-facing, two-story classroom area, the entire building was designed as a one-story structure integrating a gymnasium and school building into a rectangular plan. The height and shape of the roof were varied to give the building a distinctive character, and the gymnasium was treated as a large classroom. The focus of the children's space is the Field of Light, which is an atrium space with a skylight installed on the north side. Here, a sequence of slats reflects the natural light from the skylight and guides it inside the building.

Location: Numata, Hokkaido, Japan
Architect: Atelier BNK
Year of Completion: 2013

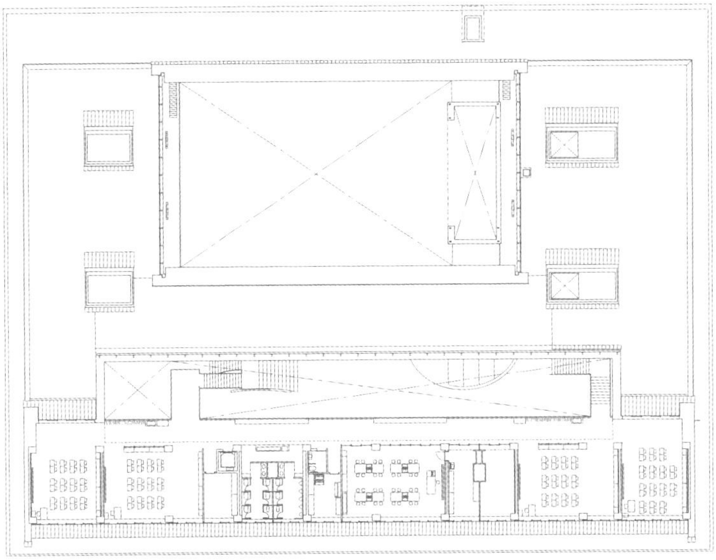

First floor plan

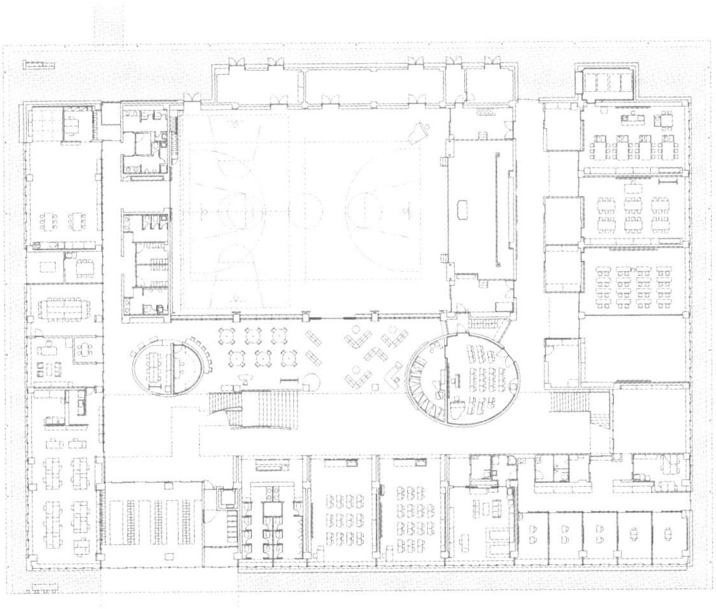

Ground floor plan

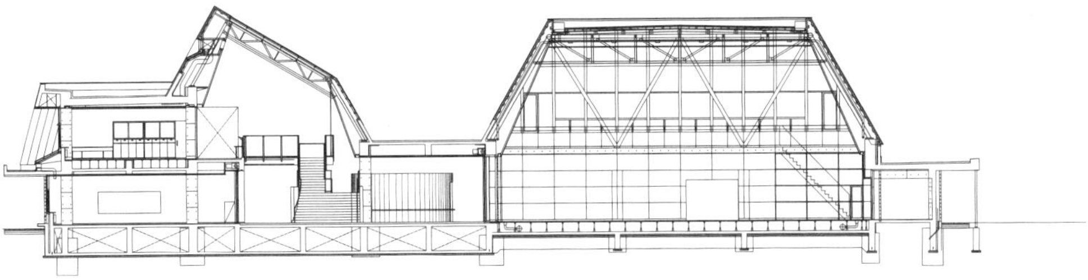

Section

West side view and school yard

East side view

Field of Light

Contrasting materials

Southern view and entrance

by Chamberlin, Powell and Bon

Barbican Centre

During the Second World War, an air raid destroyed a site, known as the Barbican, at the heart of London. A housing scheme was put forward by Chamberlin, Powell and Bon in 1955 that was intended to reverse the population decline in the area. Although the concrete at the Barbican was left exposed, it was not unfinished, having been pick-hammered to give it a rough, rustic appearance. The estate comprises three tower blocks, 13 terrace blocks, two "mews" and a row of townhouses. The towers' distinctive cantilevered balconies have elegantly curved tips and resemble a ship's hull. Their unique form reduces wind resistance and eases the strain on the structural frame. The long protrusions of the balconies, a design aspect recommended by the engineers, create deep eaves over the apartments below.

Location: London, England
Architect: Chamberlin, Powell and Bon
Year of Completion: 1982

View from above

Lake at the Barbican Centre

Silk Street entrance

by Landau + Kindelbacher Architekten Innenarchitekten

Grube Messel Visitor Center

The layer of oil shale functions as a genius loci and forms the graphic idea for the UNESCO World Natural Heritage Site Visitor Center at the Messel pit. Like a huge clump of earth, the monolithic outer wall building breaks out of the existing retaining wall and is oriented towards the quarry – the fossil site and the visitor center's main attraction. This perceived outwards-moving motion of the outer walls culminates in a projecting viewing platform with views across the research site. Visitors are taken on a symbolic tour of the earth's layers that enters a unique spatial composition. The building itself is tailored to suit the exhibition and its specific requirements. Simple yet effective architectural methods have been implemented to achieve this, such as narrow and expansive spaces, light and dark effects and high or low ceiling heights.

Location: Messel, Germany
Architect: Landau + Kindelbacher Architekten Innenarchitekten
Year of Completion: 2010

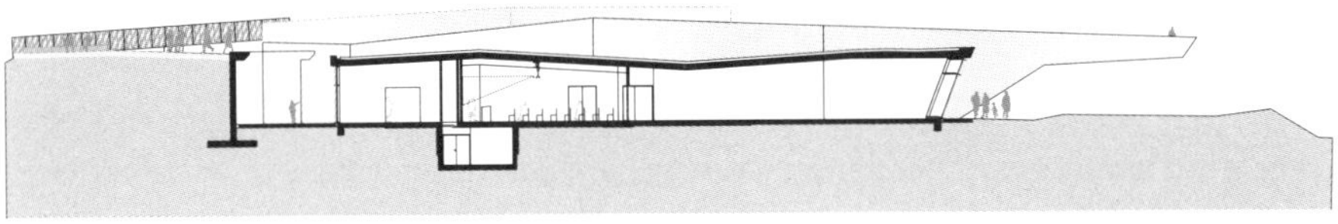

Section

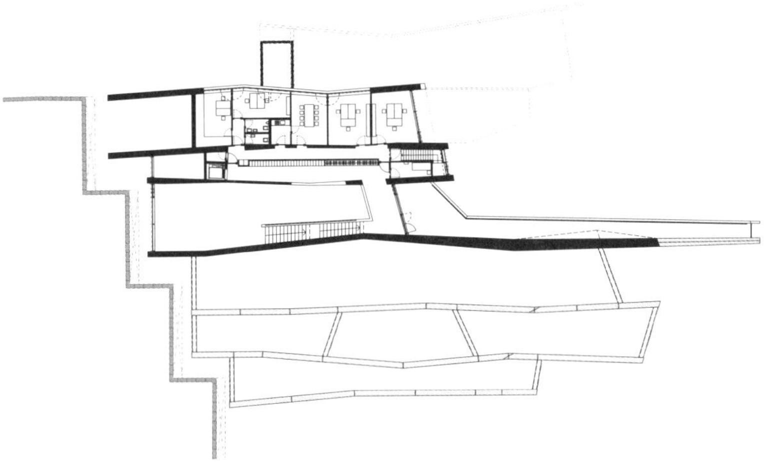

First floor plan

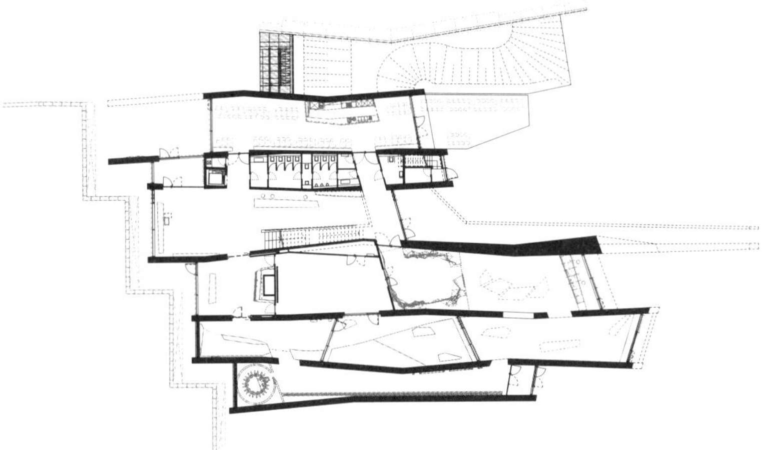

Ground floor plan

Entrance to visitor center

Wall layers representing the earth's layers

Light and dark effects at entrance

Monolithic outer wall

Viewing platform

Entrance hall

by gpy arquitectos

Faculty of Fine Arts La Laguna University

Located in a heterogeneous area, adjacent to the island highway, the new Faculty of Fine Arts building wraps itself around an intimate open space, creating an interior landscape. The building is dominated by structured concrete: a skin of suspended concrete slats adopts a curved shape and wraps and protects the interior open space of the building. The concrete skin manifests a dual vocation of scale, housing the teaching areas, offering flexible and innovative spaces for an experimental education, while at the same time defining the building's urban and territorial image. The space between the concrete skin and a continuous skin of cast glass acts like a filter, separating the spaces of specific uses from the common ones like the patio gardens and open ramps, the covered galleries and the entrance terrace.

Location: La Laguna, Tenerife, Spain
Architect: gpy arquitectos / Juan Antonio González, Urbano Yanes, Constanze Sixt
Year of Completion: 2014

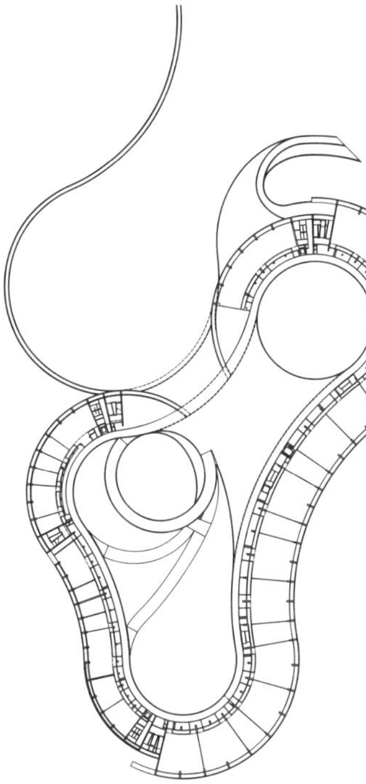

Floor plan of main entrance

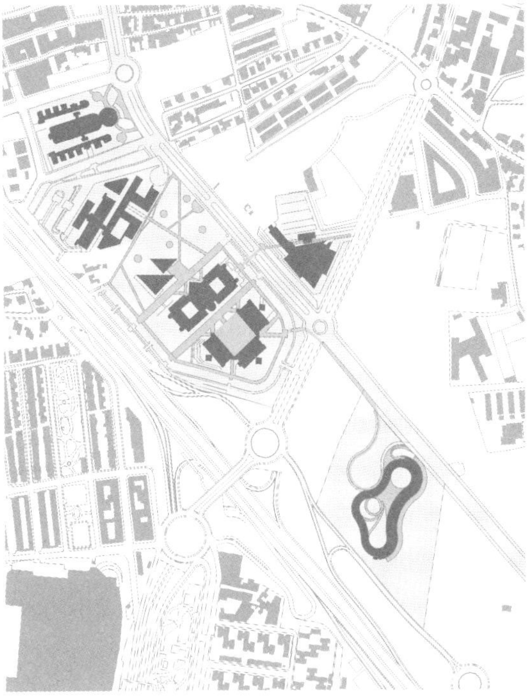

Site plan

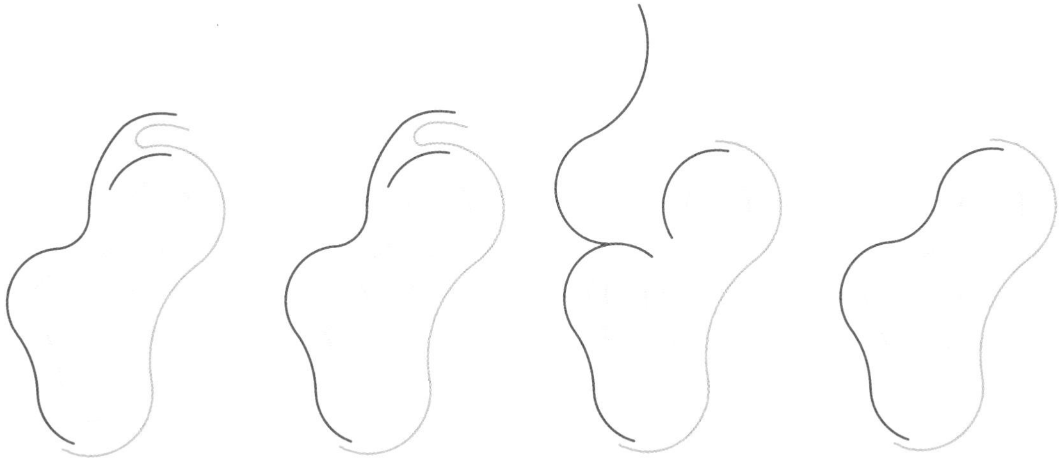

Diagrams of concrete skin (level 1–4)

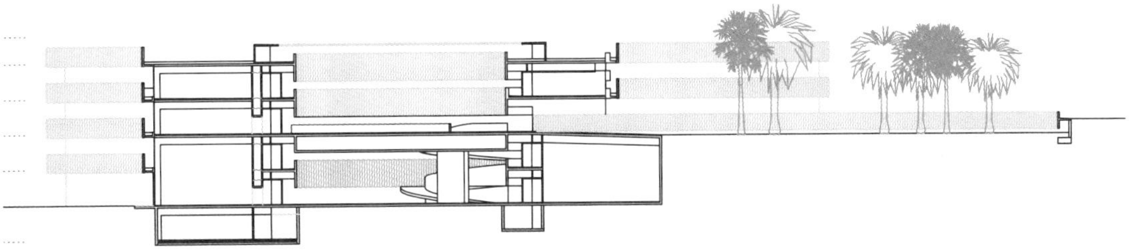

Section

Patio with central ramp

Entrance terrace

Atelier

Terrace as open corridor

Interior patio

Public plaza and main entrance

by William Pereira

Geisel Library

The Geisel Library at the University of California is located at the interface between brutalism and futurism, a position that the architect, William Pereira, intrepidly pursued throughout his career. With its strong concrete piers and hovering glassy enclosures, the library somehow manages to appear solid yet lightweight. The library is located at the geometric center of the San Diego campus, at the crest of a small canyon and is arguably the most prominent building on the campus. Eight stories in height, the building has two submerged floors and six floors of varying sizes above ground level. The treatment of the windows allows them to dematerialize into the sky, intensifying the levitating effect created by the unconventional configuration of the building.

Location: University of California, San Diego, CA, USA
Architect: William Pereira
Year of Completion: 1970

Floor supporting beams

Stories of different size

by Sophus Søbye Architects

Scout House Hindemosehus

This new scout cabin in Odense comprises two separate buildings united by a closed courtyard. One of the buildings is approximately 200 square meters and contains a tipi, café, modern kitchen and two toilets with access from outside. The other building is approximately 100 square meters and contains the patrol rooms for the older scouts as well as the leader and administration rooms. The courtyard functions as a "base camp" positioned between the buildings and partially roofed with laminated wood beams that span the space. The cabin is built of in-situ concrete sandwich walls up to four meters in height with board formwork inside and panel formwork outside. The smallest building with a sloping roof has a green roof covered with moss and other plants. Rainwater is led off the roof down the façades via recesses in the concrete that are lined with zinc.

Location: Odense, Denmark
Architect: Sophus Søbye Architects
Year of Completion: 2007

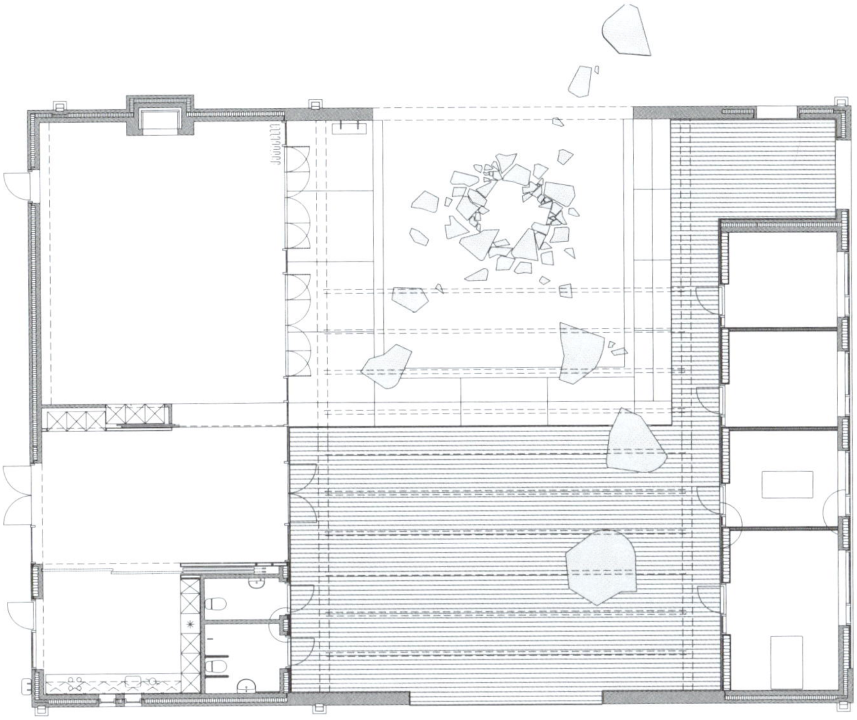

Floor plan

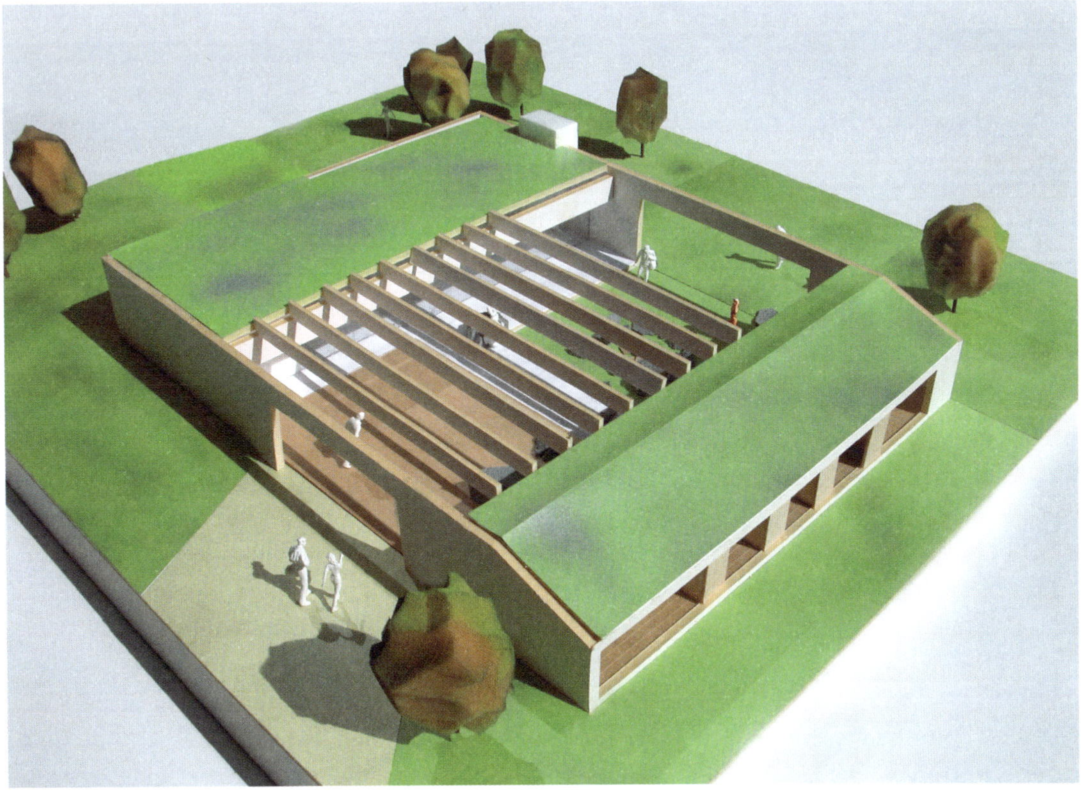

Model

Courtyard functions as a base camp

Window detail

Door detail

Courtyard roofed with laminated wood beams

Outdoor space

by Jean Balladur

La Grande-Motte

This new city with a marina, holiday homes and camping sites in the dunes of the Mediterranean was developed from nothing during the 1960s. On a 1,200-hectar site near Montpellier, Jean Balladur built a series of pyramid-shaped high-rises. His design was inspired by the pre-Colombian pyramids of Teotihuacàn in Mexico, Le Corbusier's buildings in the Indian city of Chandigarh and Oscar Niemeyer's buildings in Brasilia. The architect was fascinated by concrete and its free-formability. He used it to design balcony balustrades and façade elements that lent his up to 15-story buildings a playful, lightweight character. Balladur designed everything in La Grande-Motte: the houses, streets and sidewalks, lampposts and signage, even the traffic lights.

Location: La Grande-Motte, France
Architect: Jean Balladur
Year of Completion: 1982

Variations of graphic patterns decorate the buildings

Façade structure imitating waves

Pyramid-shaped high-rise

Scheduled Track
Work

CHAPTER 4

Clear Structure

Columns
Pillars
Beams
Patterns
Prefab

As Simon Henley writes in *Redefining Brutalism* on page 19, one of the most important defining characteristics of a brutalist building for Banham is that "imageability" must be achieved without relying on Neo-Palladian architectural forms. In 1966, Banham also explained that brutalist buildings must not be "classical" in form. He considered the Economist building by the Smithsons in London (1960–1964) to be the end of brutalism due to the "[Details of] columns in the piazza", according to an image caption on page 190 – although these were actually neither columns nor round pillars but lisenes simply added to the skeleton structure. This emphasis on vertical structuring is neither Palladian nor classical but even in the arrangement of the three building volumes he recognized that it was based on "an ancient Greek acropolis plan" (p. 134). However, he does agree with the Smithsons in *Parallel of Life and Art* where they state, "We are not going to talk about proportion and symmetry." (p. 46). When one considers the Hunstanton School, one sees immediately that the proportions could be miesian, but they are not because the regular sequence of pillars is missing. Pillars are only placed where required and there is no regular structuring. This was preferred by Banham, who demanded a "clear structure" but maintained that the arrangement should avoid classical or Palladian structuring. If one looks at the buildings from 1966 that Banham uses as examples, this type of wall structuring is accompanied by varying balconies, as seen on the Unitè, but the horizontal terraces are missing that were discussed in the last chapter as a way of distributing the building mass.

As an example, Banham also uses the Lijnbaan in Rotterdam (1949–1953) by Johannes Hendrik van

Egon Eiermann, Horten department store, Trier, 1960
The Horten-tiles are conceived as an H for the company name.

Page 182: Harry Weese, Metro, Washington D.C., 1976

den Broek and Jacob "Jaap" Bakema – who were described as "heroes" by Peter Smithson (Banham 1966, p. 45). This expands on the ideas of spatiality that characterize the Dutch De Stijl group. More than any other object, the Rietveld Chair clearly shows the connection between slats and boards that reflect the endless levels in a space. In case of Lijnbaan, pillars adopt this technique and the wall sections look as if they have simply been screwed on, almost as an afterthought. The contrast between the wall and floor orientations on the one hand, and pillars/beams/girders on the other hand can be seen in numerous brutalist buildings. Kenzo Tange's Kagawa Prefectural Office in Takamatsu, 1958 also demonstrates this principle, where structuring is provided by supporting elements such as girders. This is often seen in large-scale apartment buildings. The ends of girders and floor plates can often be seen penetrating the façade and projecting out further than necessary. This gives the observer a heightened understanding of the supporting structure, as if the building is simply made of individual elements that have been plugged together. The technique of making structural elements visible in this way can also be seen in the design of the L'Istituto Marchiondi Spagliardi in Milan by Vittoriano Viganò (1960), where the structure projects out away from the building volume. Regardless of whether these have classic or Palladian proportions, they definitely display the desired "clear structure".

Brutalism as we understand it today demonstrates far more wall structuring techniques. One of the most popular of these techniques is the use of ornamental surfaces – although the use of the word "ornamental" would almost certainly have been rejected at the time. A precursor of this trend was Perret's Notre-Dame in Raincy. By freeing the walls of their load-bearing duties, he was able to integrate prefabricated glazed concrete elements of 60 × 60 centimeters that only had to support themselves. Marcel Lambrich's façade for the former Credit Communal in Brussels (1969–1974) was covered by large three-pronged decorative elements balanced one above the other, Egon Eiermann (approx. 1960) covered the Horten chain of department stores with glazed Horten-tiles that he designed himself. He used these to cover the entrance façade with a ceramic wallpaper that had a depth of 15–20 centimeters. For the Berlin Memorial Church, Eiermann filled the empty space between, not in front of, the static system the way Hunstanton does with brick infill – but in such cases the architect nevertheless has the opportunity to develop the pattern between the static elements as he wishes. In the case of Perret's church and the Horten department stores, the structural supports are positioned behind the wall, so that the

Marcel Lambrichs, Credit Communal, Brussels, 1973
Heavy prefab Ys standing on one another in front of the windows.

Kenzo Tange, Kagawa Prefectural Office, Takamatsu, 1958
Reinforced concrete emulates traditional Japanese wooden architecture.

patterns or structuring used on the façade can be developed without any interruptions.
After 1945, architectural designs for department stores began to avoid the use of windows, as this meant that the goods could be better presented using artificial light. Because of this, numerous similar solutions were developed as the windowless façades had larger surfaces and fewer interruptions. The patterns and solutions used became more sculptural and ingenious, for example the use of an aluminum honeycomb-like pattern on the Centrum Warenhaus in Dresden, designed by Hungarians Ferenc Simon and Ivan Fokvari and built by Werner Wunderwald and G. Trepte (1973–1978). This was torn down in 2007. A precursor to this design was the temporary pavilion "Wehrhafte Schweiz" by Carl Fingerhuth at the Swiss National Exhibition in 1964 in Lausanne, where crystal-like spikes were intended to demonstrate the country's defensive potential. Folded structures were rarely used to structure façades – although one example of where this was the case is St. Paulus in Neuss-Weckhoven by Fritz and Christian Schalle (1966–1968) and Tange's Town Hall in Imabari (1957–1959) – it was much more commonly used as a roof motif.
The use of a sculptural, repetitive façade pattern was also commonly used for parking lots (Welbeck Street Car Park in London by Michael Blampied, 1969; Prince Street Car Park in Bristol by Kenneth Wakeford Jarram & Harris, 1966) and is currently gaining in popularity once more (Charles Street Car Park by Allies & Morrison, 2008) mainly due to technological advancements. Such façade elements can be utilized as high-tech shading solutions on tall buildings, for example the Al Bahr Towers in Abu Dhabi by Aedes, 2012.

Even large-scale façade elements – the worst examples of this are the typical prefabricated buildings that were common in the GDR – belong to the category of façade structuring through repetition, albeit a boring structural technique. However, there are better ways of using prefabricated elements, as Banham demonstrates with the example of a residential building by Vladimir Bodiansky and ATBAT-Afrique in Algeria (begun in 1963), where the balconies projecting out from the building face form a series of cubes across two levels, similar to Francisco and Manuel Aires Mateus' much-praised House for Elderly People in Alcacer do Sal, 2010. Various buildings by Georges Candilis in Casablanca like the Sidi Othman Apartment Buildings (1953) also use this technique, where rectangular balconies structure the façade. These look like a more tidy version of Habitat 67 by Safdie. These are not mentioned by Banham, but are referred to by Jürgen Joedicke in an article published in 1964. The projecting and cantilevered elements are intended to serve shading needs.

Peter and Alison Smithson, Robin Hood Gardens, London, 1972
Two broad "Streets in the Sky" characterize this residential estate.

The same applies for Zvi Hecker's Dubiner Apartment House in Ramat Gan, 1961–1963, that can be recognized as a forerunner to the disorder of Habitat 67, but really are more an example of projections and recesses, as also often seen in work by MVRDV.

However, overhanging terraces, recessed levels and loggia or balconies have become much more common as structural elements following the design of the Unité. That these techniques were not always successful is demonstrated by the controversial design of the Robin Hood Gardens in London by the Smithsons (1969–1972). This was torn down in 2017. Other examples include the apartment buildings in Bijlmermeer in Amsterdam, headed by Siegfried Nassut; or the 33 Pruitt-Igoe Buildings in St. Louis, MO, by Minoru Yamasaki (1956). Charles Jencks wrote about the 1972 demolition of these in *The Language of Post-Modern Architecture* on page 9, "Happily, it is possible to date the death of Modern Architecture to a precise moment in time."

Another form of structuring that deserves a brief mention here is ceiling structuring, often done by making the substructure visible. This can be developed into a strikingly decorative design with opulent patterns, as seen in Kahn's design of the Yale University Art Gallery in New Haven, CT.

Oscar Niemeyer, Supreme Federal Court, Brasilia, 1957
A regular structure of pillars, but not classical.

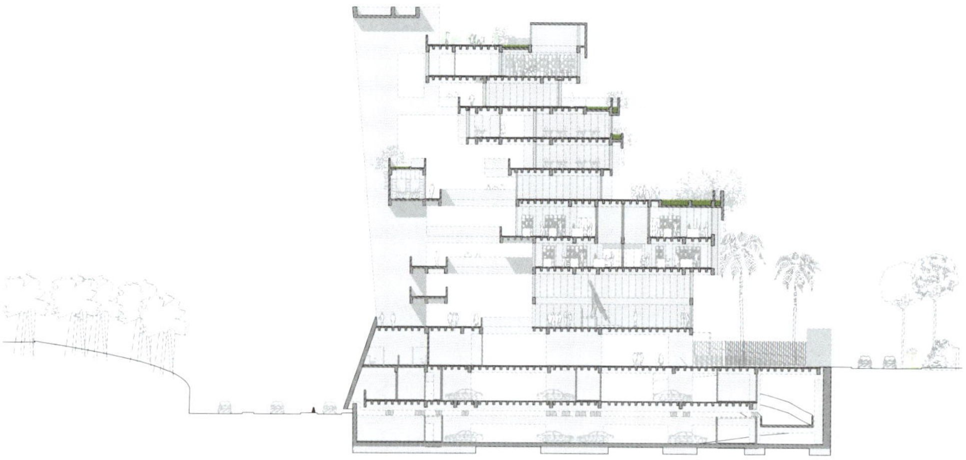

Section

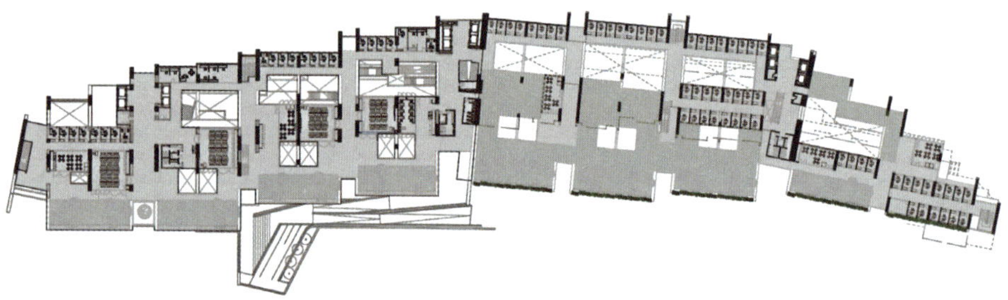

Fifth floor plan – phase I and II

Third floor plan – phase I and II

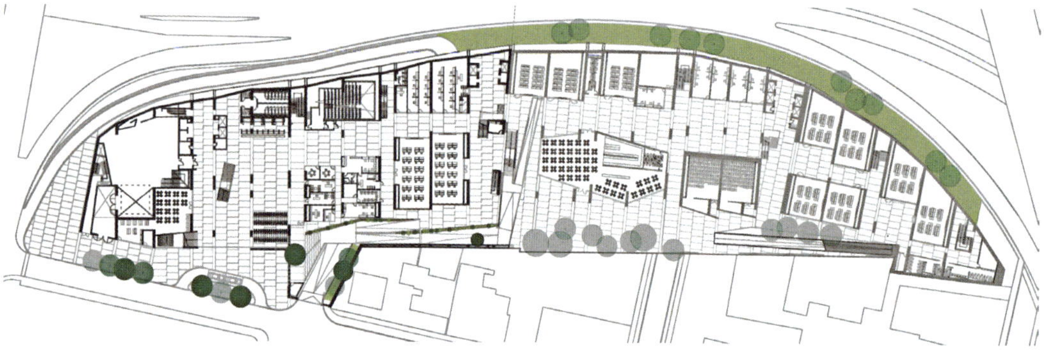

Ground floor plan – phase I and II

by Grafton Architects

University Campus UTEC Lima

Architects need to reassess their impact on the earth. Rather than thinking of buildings as isolated objects, these architects think about buildings as New Geography, creating an infrastructure for life. While the north face of the campus acts as "cliff" or "shoulder" to the fast-moving city, the architects have terraced the lecture rooms, laboratories and teaching spaces, so that their roofs become cascading gardens, reminiscent of the cultivated terraces of Machu Picchu. The landscape has been woven into the building. In terms of education, the strategy connects the ground and sky. The larger volumes have been placed near to the ground, with the teaching spaces and administration area located above. The in-situ, reinforced concrete building is organized by a 20-meter main structure and a 10-meter intermediate structural grid.

Location: Lima, Peru
Architect: Grafton Architects
Year of Completion: 2015

Street façade

In-situ reinforced concrete structure

Main and intermediate structural grid

View from the valley

Cascading gardens

View to residential block

Buidlings as seen from St James's Street

Economist building

Steps to plaza

by Alison and Peter Smithson

Economist Building

In 1960, the British business paper the The Economist planned the construction of a new editorial office in London. The office building was completed in 1964 and comprises three buildings, all grouped around a pedestrian plaza that is reached by integrated stairs or a gentle ramp from street level. The complex is devised of a four-story irregular polygon block on St James's Street, a main tower of 15 stories and an eight-story residential block. Each of the buildings is articulated with bold uprights running from the top of the buildings to the ground floor. At ground level, recesses and incisions at the corners allow light to flow inside. The buildings have a light façade, made using a type of fossil-rich Portland stone. In the visual arts wing, large windows and skylights provide the maximum amount of natural light.

Location: London, England
Architect: Alison and Peter Smithson
Year of Completion: 1964

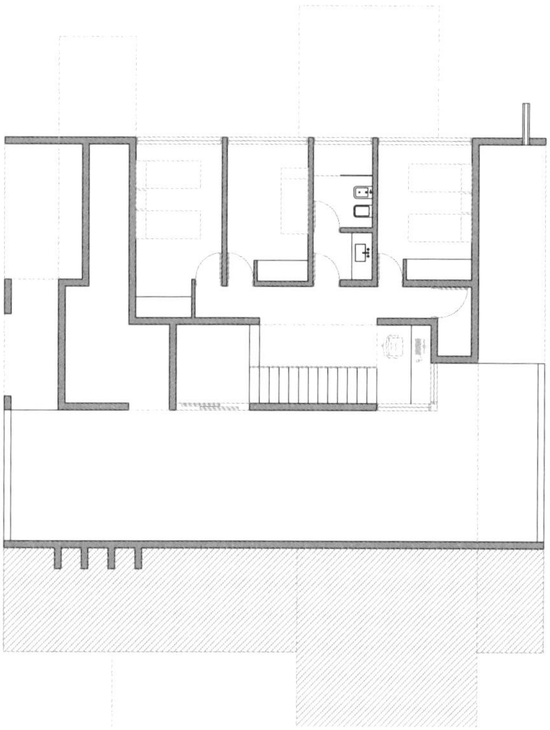

Lower level plan

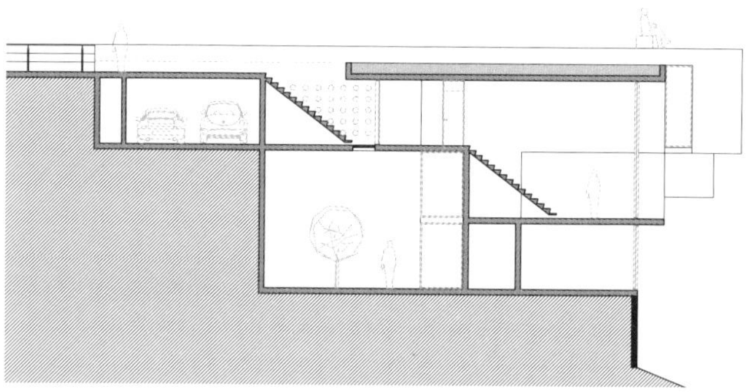

Section

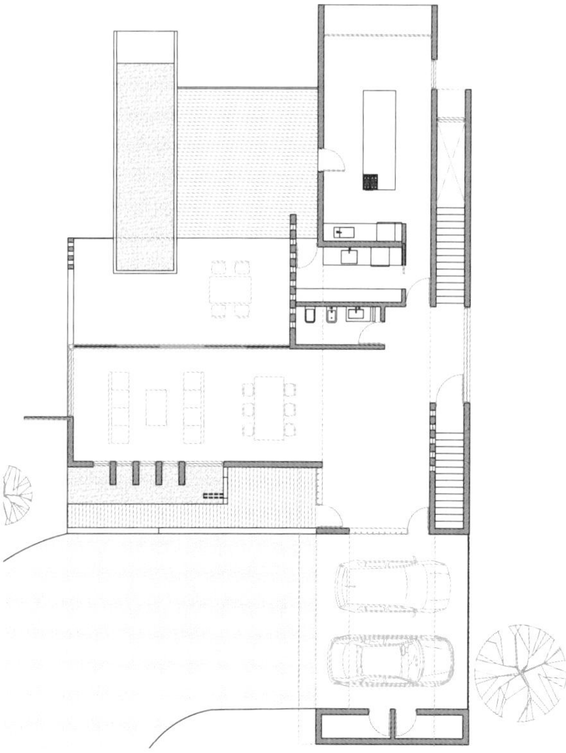

Upper level plan

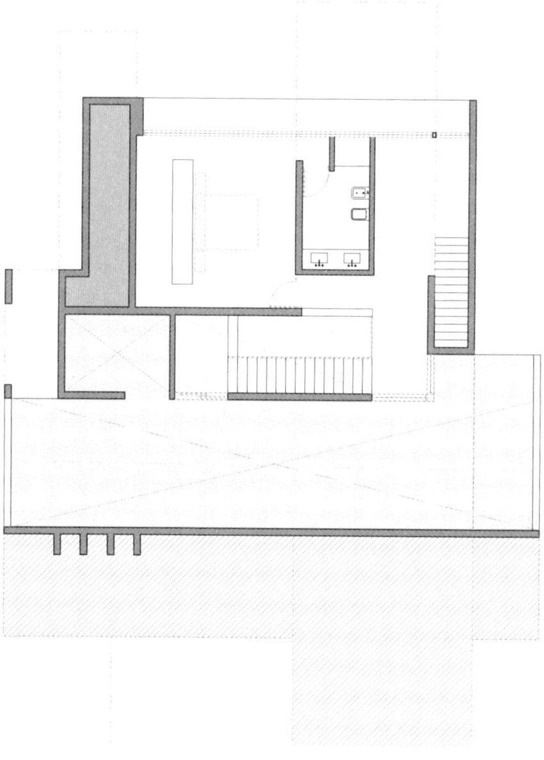

Intermediate level plan

by Agustín Lozada

La Cuesta House

La Cuesta House is located within the Sierras Chicas hills, a few kilometers away from Córdoba, Argentina. Lying above the rough slopes, this house fuses the architecture and the land by integrating a number of open spaces. The 380-square-meter building is organized into three stories to accommodate the abrupt decline. Access to the house is provided via a pedestrian bridge that connects the street with the upper terrace. The upper floor hosts the social activities and offers the best views, while the middle floor houses the main bedroom, and the lower floor the secondary bedrooms and a playroom. The main materials chosen include reinforced concrete and local rock to cause the lowest possible natural impact. Water features is a key feature of the outdoor areas.

Location: La Calera, Córdoba, Argentina
Architect: Agustín Lozada
Year of Completion: 2015

Upper level and entrance

View from below

Pool on roof

Access at upper level

Upper level interior space

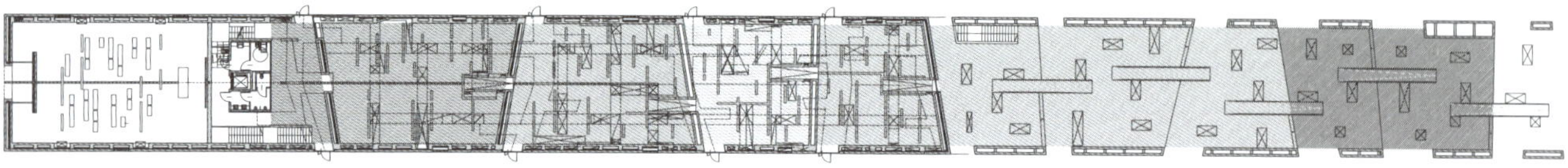

First floor

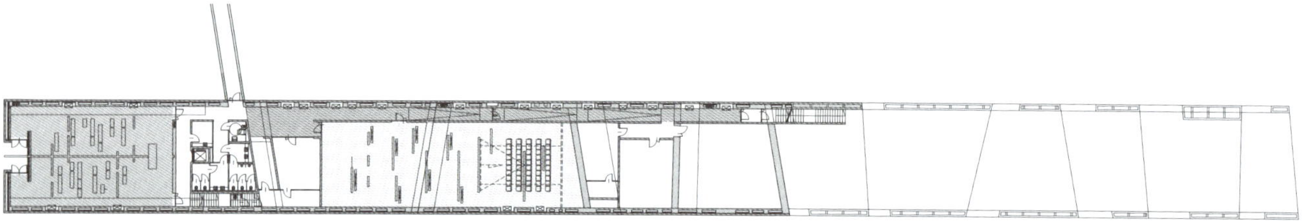

Ground floor

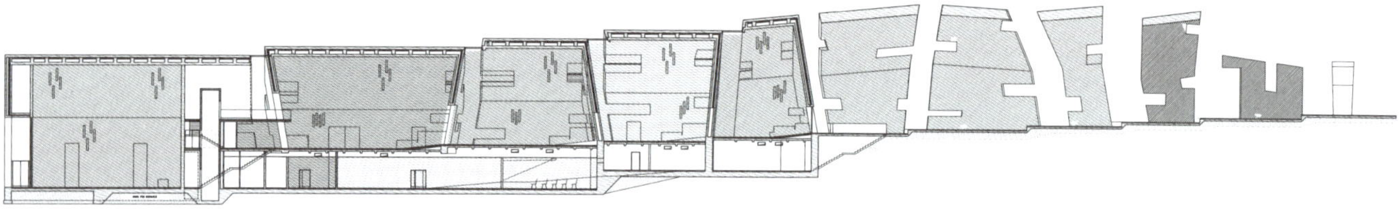

Longitudinal section

Pilaster rise from slab foundation to form the roof

by Nizio Design International, Miroslaw Nizio

Mausoleum in Michniów

The Mausoleum of the Martyrdom of Polish Villages in Michniów, designed by Mirosław Nizio, is a monolithic sculptural form that provides space for a multimedia exhibition. The shape of the building conveys the dramaturgy of the historical developments – Michniów itself is a symbol of all village pacifications that took place during World War II. The object's monolithic structure was designed by applying watertight concrete jointing and injection technology. The building has a characteristic segmented structure, its fabric is cut across by incisions that divide the architectural form into closed and open parts. This is the result of sculptural inspirations and the importance of linking the architecture with the historical narrative. The overall surface of the layout exceeds 16,200 square meters.

Location: Michniów, Poland
Architect: Nizio Design International, Mirosław Nizio
Year of Completion: 2017

Entrance with "Pieta of Michniów"-sculpture by Wacław Stawecki (1993)

Surfaces of ferroconcrete elements reproduce the structural features of wood

Open segments

Folding ferroconcrete

Five closed and six open segments queuing up

The façade is made of framed stained glass inlays

New tower and chapel next to the old tower

Inside the new church

by Egon Eiermann

Kaiser Wilhelm Memorial Church

This church ensemble is a peace memorial. The 71-meter tower of the Neo-Romanesque church that was destroyed during the Second World War is surrounded by a four-part building ensemble built of concrete, steel and glass: an octagonal church nave, a rectangular foyer, a 53.5-meter square bell tower and a square single-story chapel. The grid walls of the buildings comprise more than 20,000 glass pieces in total. These are embedded into the façade's steel construction. Extra-strong ultramarine blue glass has been used, smashed to form irregular small sections and then arranged to fit the square frames and embedded into the concrete grid. Inside, this gives the impression that one is sitting in a blue polished gemstone.

Location: Berlin, Germany
Architect: Egon Eiermann
Year of Completion: 1961

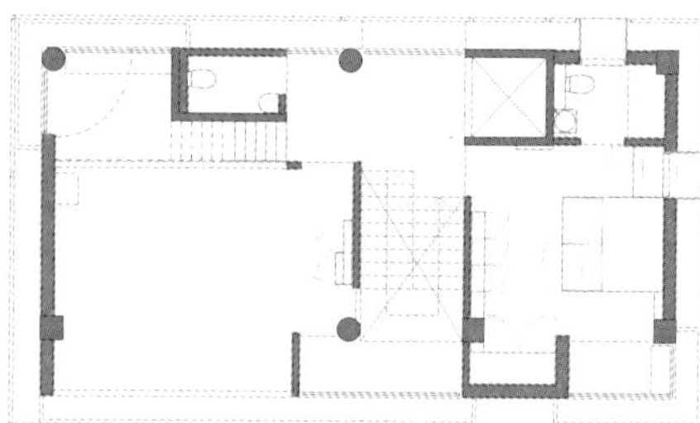

Fourth floor plan

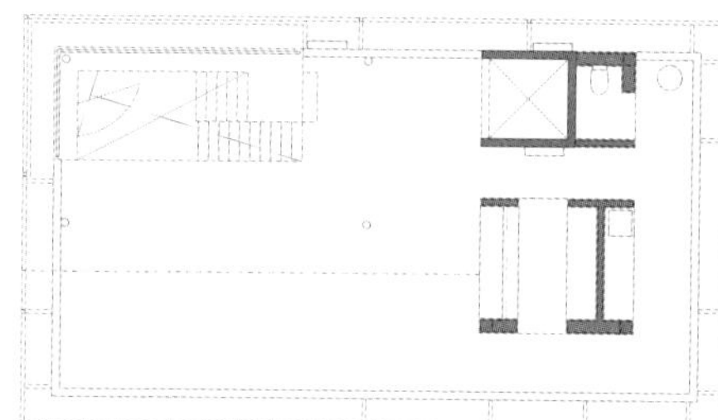

Fifth floor plan

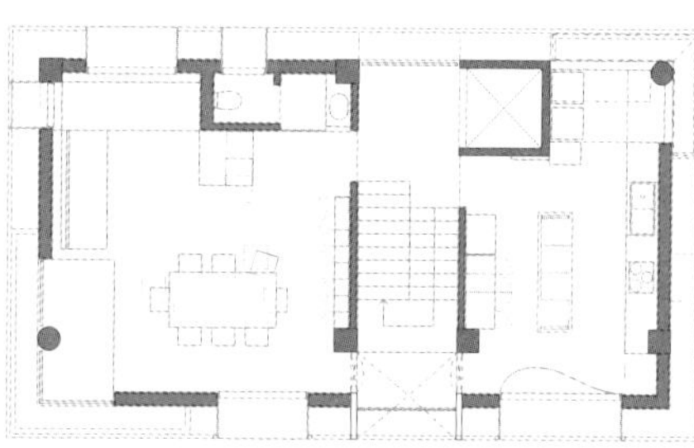

Second floor plan

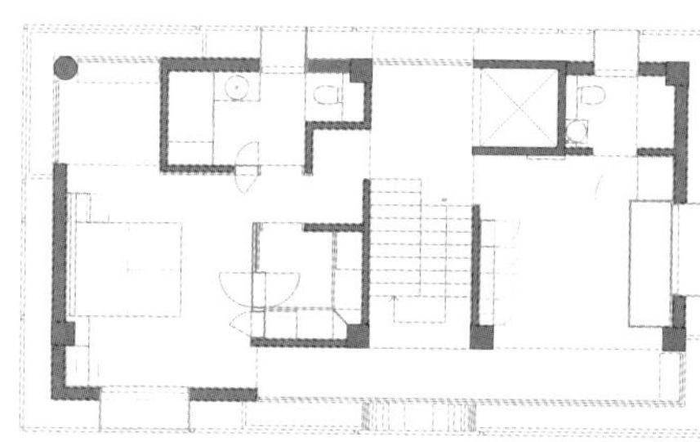

Third floor plan

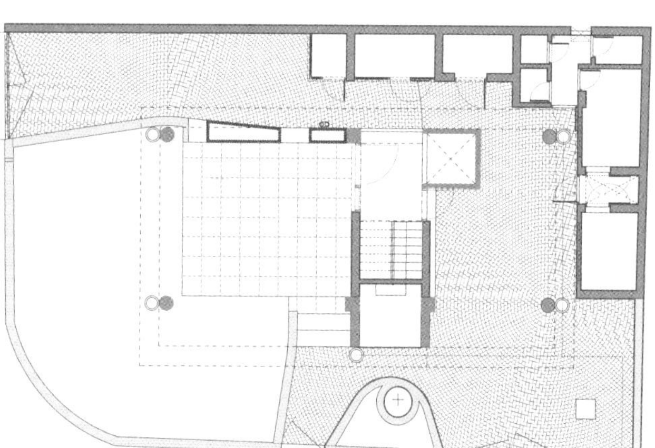

Ground floor plan

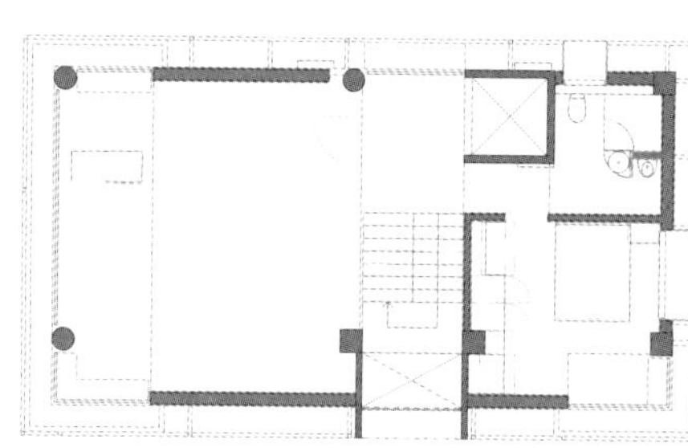

First floor plan

by banduk smith studio

Tower House

Tower House is an experiment in vertical living. A typical bungalow of 345 square meters has been squeezed into a footprint of just 6.5 x 12.5 meters, forcing the program to develop vertically rather than horizontally. The architects intended to create a space that evokes the warmth and connection of shared spaces and creates a wealth of different experiences spread throughout the space. The verticality also offers a number of advantages, facilitating the efficiency of plumbing and mechanical systems and providing views across the city. The arrangement also makes clever use of stack and cross ventilation. Structural support is provided by a concrete frame. The balconies have been given a different position on each floor to make the most of the views.

Location: Ahmedabad, India
Architect: banduk smith studio
Year of Completion: 2015

View from below

Lower balcony

Balconies wrap around the façade

Ceramic brick screen

Lower balcony in landscape

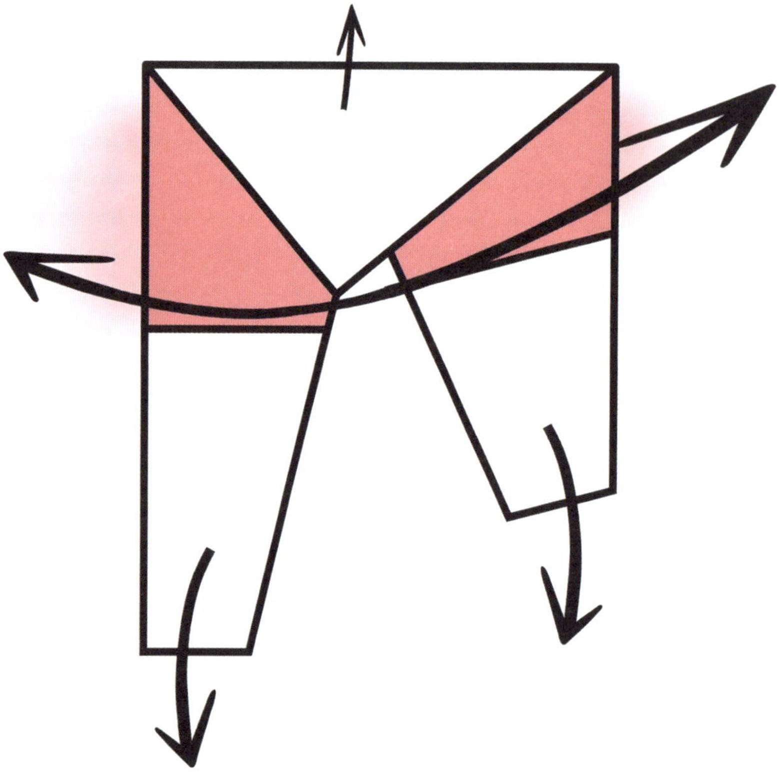

Flow of movement

Interior design by Martha Perez

by Cadaval & Solà-Morales

MA House

For the design of this house, the clients requested that stone be used as the main construction material. This decision was not made for esthetic reasons, but because of maintenance requirements and the low price per square meter. MA House is located on the outskirts of Tepoztlán, a small picturesque village with a colonial urban center. Located 60 kilometers from Mexico City, Tepoztlán is known for its sunny weather, a comfortable temperature all year long and its lush vegetation. The house is organized as a succession of spaces that serve different uses and define the outer boundary, a generic geometrical square. The design is characterized by a sequence of open and closed areas, including roofed patios that intersect diagonally with the volume and break the rigidity of the perimeter.

Location: Tepoztlán, Mexico
Architect: Cadaval & Solà-Morales
Year of Completion: 2016

Exterior contrasts solid and glazed areas

Interior with intermediate level

View from open to closed space

Exterior in context

Sequence of closed and open spaces

Roofed patio

Passageway and steps to the entrance

Front façade

Library extension with decorative screens

by Paul Rudolph

Jewett Arts Center Wellesley College

The Jewett Arts Center at Wellesley College was the first major building erected by the distinguished American architect Paul Rudolph. In terms of its appearance, it has more in common with a simple orthogonal box than his later more monumental and sculptural buildings. The main exterior material is brick, matched in color to the brick of the surrounding structures. In addition, the concrete copings and clustered columns are reminiscent of the Gothic style of the adjacent buildings. The building is composed of three sections: two wings, one devoted to the visual arts and one to the performing arts, are bridged by an exhibition gallery. The large windows of the visual arts wing are shaded by porcelain-on-aluminum grilles. The performing arts wing does not use glass on the same scale, it has a much more solid and introverted structure.

Location: Wellesley, MA, USA
Architect: Paul Rudolph
Year of Completion: 1958

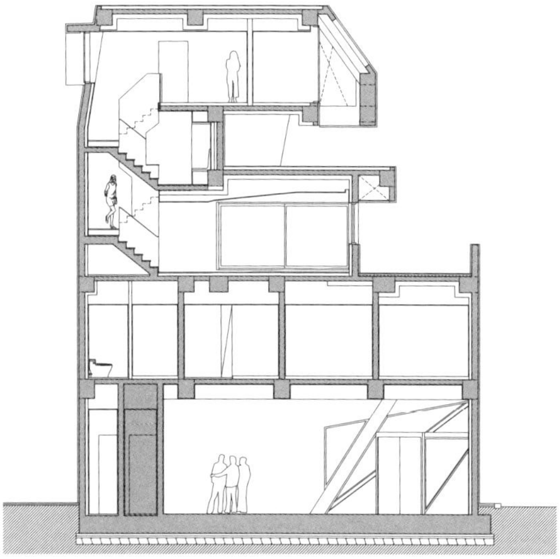
Longitudinal section

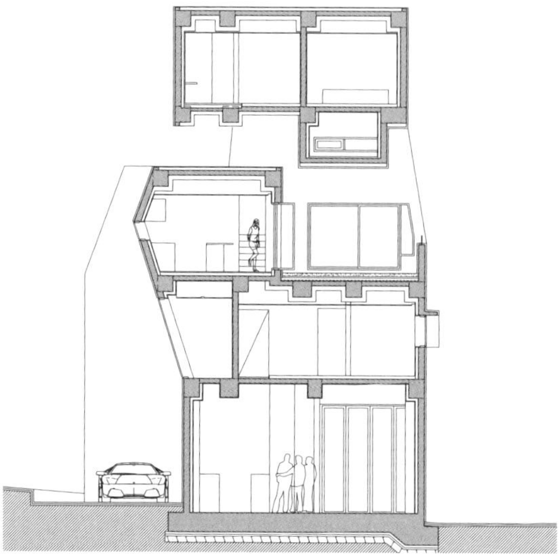
Cross section

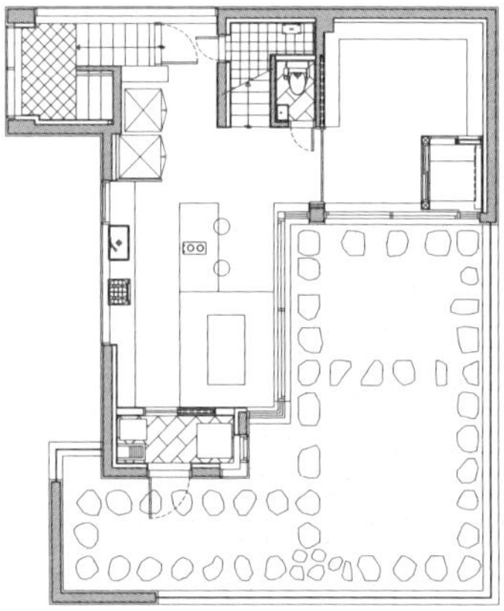
Second floor

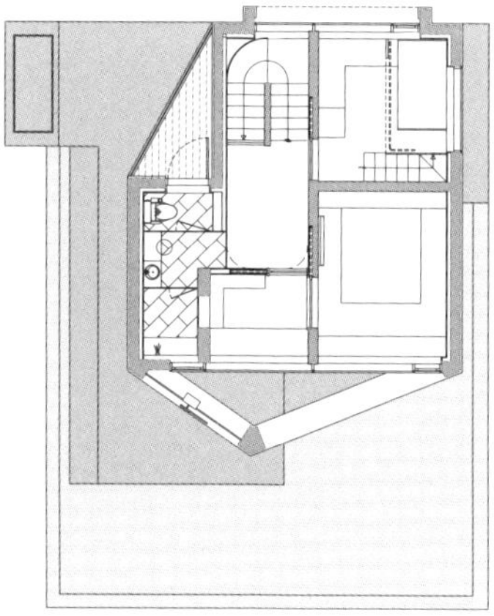
Third floor

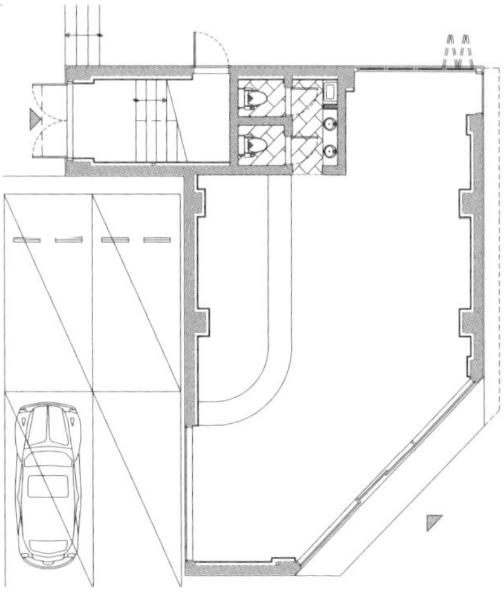
Ground floor

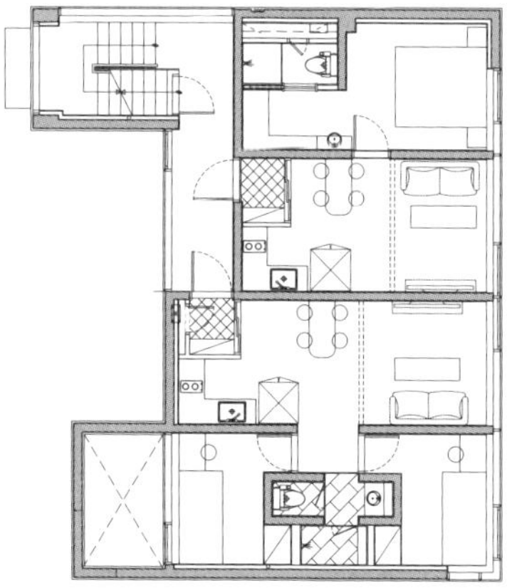
First floor

by Moon Hoon

Busan Times

This building is nicknamed The Owl. When observed from the rear, the shape of the buildings and the windows makes it appear as if the building has a large head with two eyes. Views of the night sky can be seen through a small circular skylight from the bed in the children's room at the top of the building, and the hole in the floor leads to a play space below that is not included in the building coverage or total floor area. Although the architect designed this feature with the image in mind of a child climbing down a pipe through the opening like a firefighter, this aspect was not carried out in the end as the parents had some concerns about safety. Inside, the combination of windows and openings, cleverly designed lighting concepts, light walls and wooden elements give the house a bright and modern feel.

Location: Busan, Korea
Architect: Moon Hoon
Year of Completion: 2015

View from the road

Southeast elevation

Entrance

Northwest elevation

View from the terrace

View at night

The Owl

Curving sculptural form

Building stands on pairs of pilotis

Economical modular design

by Marcel Breuer

Robert C. Weaver Federal Building

This 10-story office building, formerly known as the Department of Housing and Urban Development (HUD), was designed according to the "Guiding Principles for Federal Architecture", established by John F. Kennedy in 1962 to encourage quality modern design. The building was the first fully modular design for a federal office building and was completed significantly under budget. The mass of precast concrete as the primary structural and exterior finish material is dramatically suspended on pilotis that taper together in pairs to a narrow base at ground level, where recessed walls clad in granite create a sheltered loggia. The building was renamed in 1999 in honor of Dr. Robert C Weaver, the first Secretary of Housing and Urban Development.

Location: Washington, D.C., USA
Architect: Marcel Breuer
Year of Completion: 1968

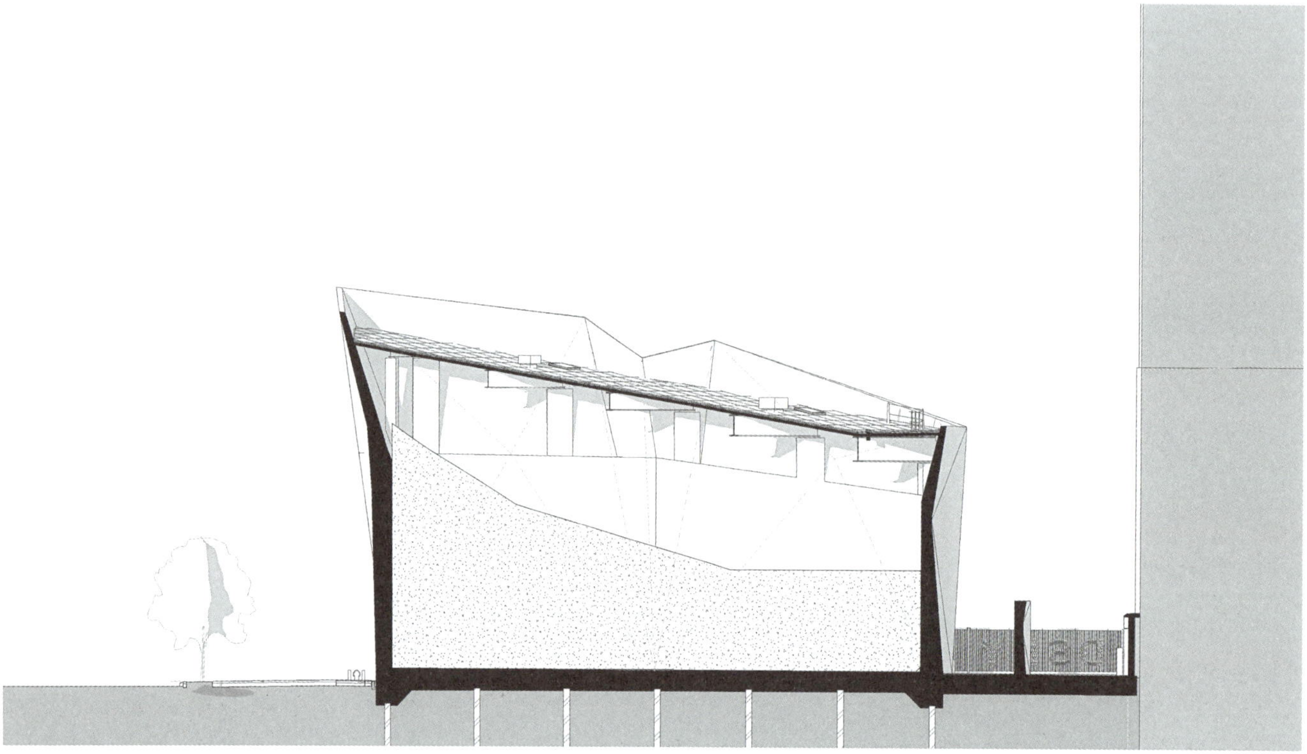

Section

Salt shed in winter

by Dattner Architects with WXY Architecture + Urban Design

Spring Street Salt Shed

Rising to a height of over 20 meters along the Hudson River, the Spring Street Salt Shed houses 5,000 tons of road salt for the New York City Department of Sanitation. Inspired by a collection of salt crystals, faceted planes enliven this highly visible structure, creating a sculptural landmark in the neighborhood. The cast-in-place concrete structure tapers toward the bottom, creating more pedestrian space beneath a dramatic overhang. The shed emerges from a moat of textured glass paving, further contributing to the enigmatic and iconic nature of this place in the city. Concrete was a natural material selection, serving as both the building structure and exterior finish, eliminating the need for additional materials. The smooth finish and light color of the concrete, which will resemble the color of salt over time with more exposure to sunlight, emphasize the form of the building.

Location: New York City, NY, USA
Architect: Dattner Architects with WXY Architecture + Urban Design
Year of Completion: 2015

Vehicle leaving the salt shed

Façade inspired by salt crystals

Façade detail

Unusual shape of the industrial building

Building provides a striking contrast to surrounding constructions

Unité d'Habitation Berlin

Roof terrace in Marseille

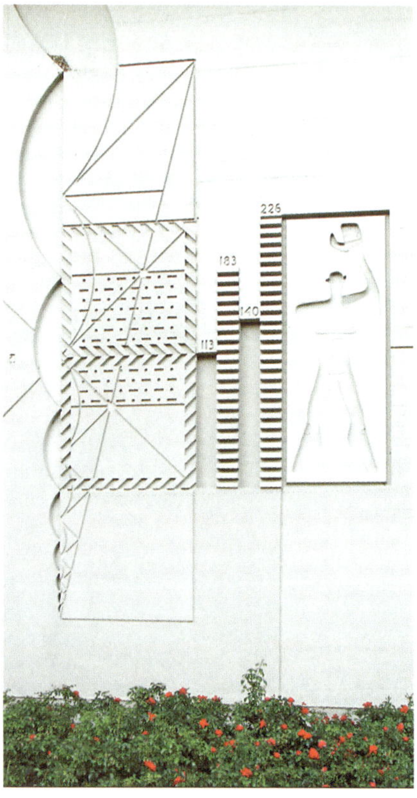

Modulor next to the entrance in Berlin

Typical "rue interieur" in Marseille

by Le Corbusier

Unité d'Habitation

The Unité d'Habitation is a design principle developed by Le Corbusier for residential housing developments. Several of these were built throughout Europe, the most famous of which is located in Marseille and was built between 1947 and 1952. This is considered enormously influential and is often said to have inspired the Brutalist style. All are constructed of rough-cast concrete to save money. Typical elements include the pilotis that free up the ground floor, and the "rue interieur". The original design drew on the duplex-flat idea of the Soviet housing project Narkomfin Building in Moscow by Moisei Ginzburg and Ignaty Milinis (1930). Unusually, the apartments were all equipped with built-in furniture and specially designed storage walls comprising various cupboards with sliding doors, designed in collaboration with Charlotte Perriand.

Location: Marseille, Nantes-Rezé, Briey, Firminy, all in France and Berlin, Germany
Architect: Le Corbusier
Year of Completion: 1952

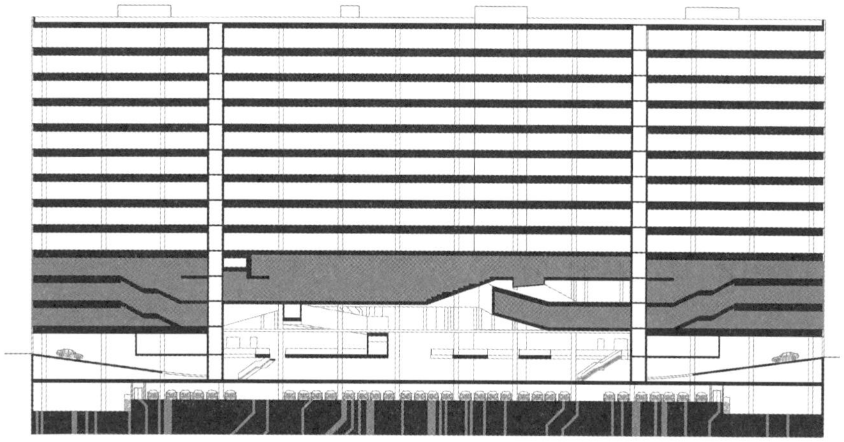

Section

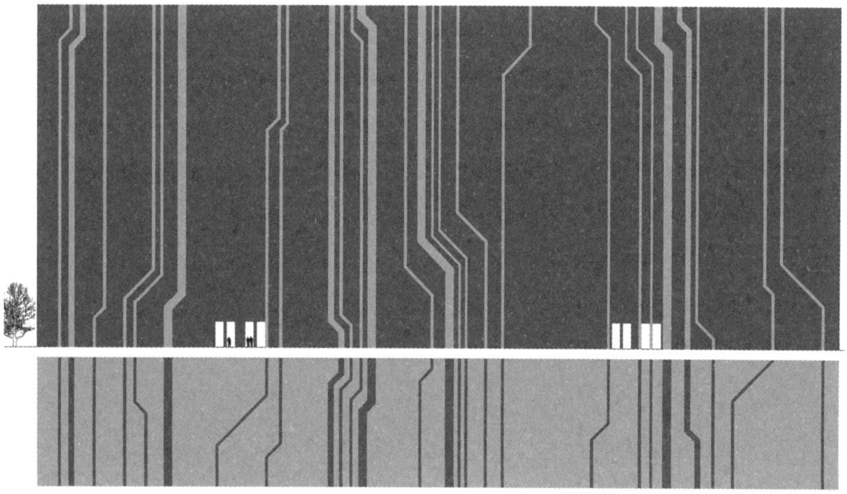

West elevation

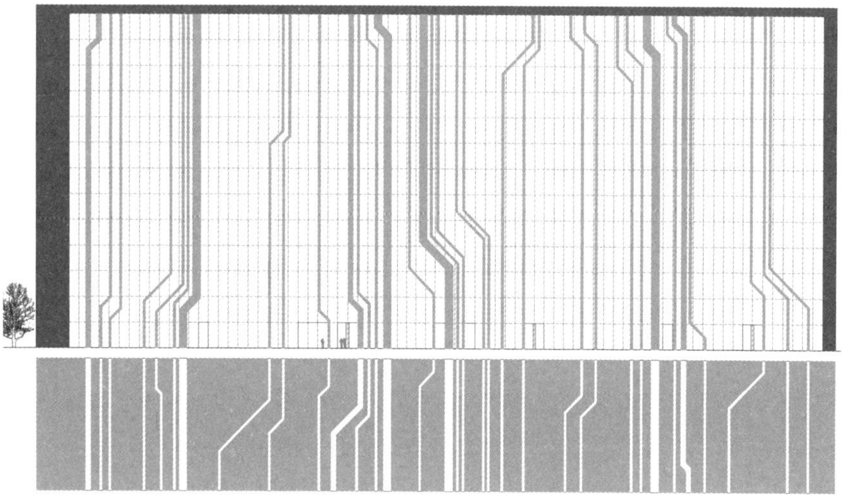

East elevation

by Studio Zhu-Pei and Urbanus

Digital Beijing

Intended as a landmark building for the Olympics, the Digital Beijing Building is located at the northern end of the central axis, neighboring the core area that housed the Olympics Center, the National Stadium and National Swimming Center. The Digital Beijing Building, nearly 100,000 square meters in area, served as the control center and the data center for the Beijing Olympics in 2008. Furthermore, it accommodated a virtual museum of Digital Olympics and an exhibition center for manufacturers of digital products. The transparent façade faces the Olympic Park, while the solid façade is oriented westwards. The details of the façades were inspired by media images to try to reveal an enlarged micro world suggestive of the microchips abundant but ignored in our daily lives.

Location: Beijing, China
Architect: Studio Zhu-Pei and Urbanus
Year of Completion: 2007

Pedestrian view

Slits in the façade inspired by microchips

Exhibition space

View from south

Solid façade facing west

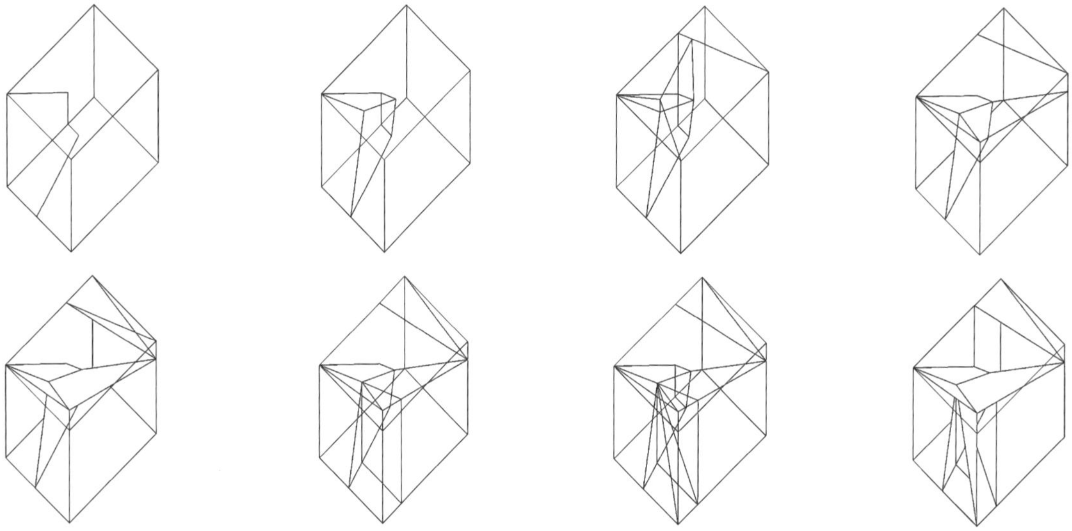

Schematic folding study

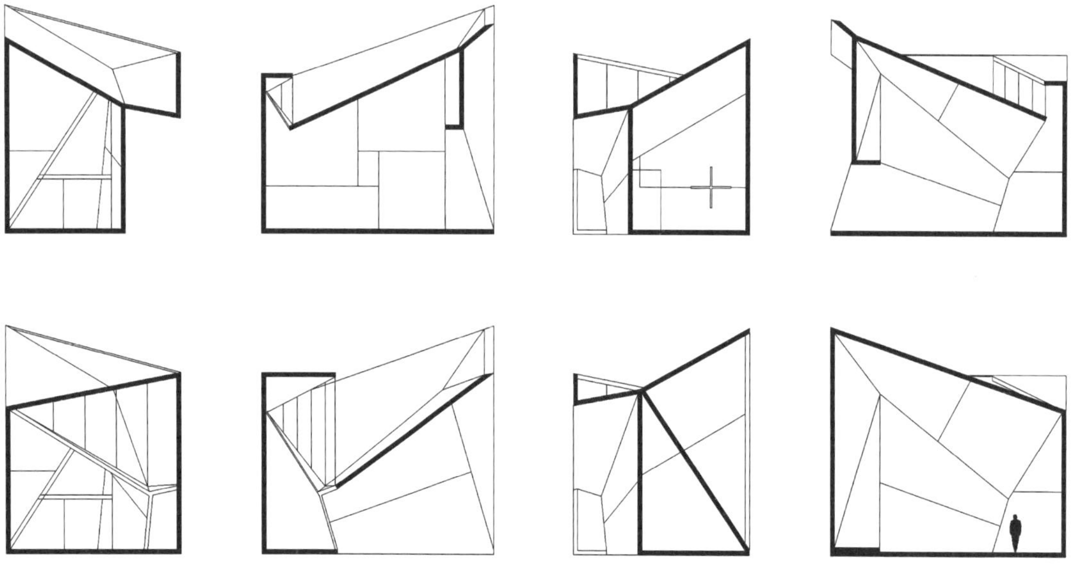

Schematic plans

by S-M.A.O.

Valleaceron Chapel

This chapel is located at the top of a slight rise – on the north slope of a low hill overlooking different landscapes. The site, the valleys and the broken, blurred horizon make the chapel the reference point in the landscape seen from the property entrance. Visitors enter the chapel via a rise in the western façade. The chapel has a naked design and no artificial lighting. The spatial relationship between exterior-interior is the focus of the design. Only a cross, an onyx lamp and an image as the focal point underscore the symbolic aspects of the project. The proposed fold in the structure, the Corbusian boîte, gives rise to a single material – concrete captures all of the nuances of the volume. Light thus takes on the role of the second material in the chapel, contrasting with the opacity of the concrete.

Location: Almadén, Ciudad Real, Spain
Architect: S-M.A.O. Sancho-Madridejos Architecture Office
Year of Completion: 2000

Building in landscape

Entrance in west façade

Light entering the room

Entrance

Folding structure

CHAPTER 5

Disposition of Space

Urban Space
Neighborhood
Privacy
Metabolism
Structuralism

In 1953, while the Hunstanton School was being built, a group of young architects at the ninth CIAM (Congrès Internationaux d'Architecture Moderne) in Aix-en-Provence were commissioned to prepare the tenth congress in Dubrovnik in 1956. This was the founding moment of Team Ten, which included the Smithsons, Aldo van Eyck, Jacob Bakema, Le Corbusier employee Georges Candilis and Shadrach Woods, as well as John Voelcker, Bill and Gill Howell. Giancarlo De Carlo later also joined the core group. This was the beginning of the end for CIAM. The preparation for the 11th congress was also supposed to be carried out by Team Ten, taking place in Otterlo in 1959, but that was the last CIAM to be held. The institution, which embodied the triumphal march of the Classical Modern like no other, came abruptly to an end.

In Aix-en-Provence the resistance from this group of young architects was focused in particular on ideas of urban development. The CIAM represented the idea of "The Functional City", and this was the theme of the fourth congress, which took place on a cruise ship in 1933 and ended with the approval of the famous Athens Charter. This charter was intended to have a significant effect on urban planning after 1945, brought about by its demand for the separation of living, working, relaxation areas and space for movement. This was seen by its supporters as being the solution to all urban problems. The most important building task was the creation of residences in satellite towns, where the car was to be afforded much more space, bringing to life the vision of Ludwig Hilberscheimer, published in 1928 in the fifth volume of the Bauhaus Books *Concrete as Form*, with raised streets for pedestrians, while cars were kept at ground level between gigantic high-rise buildings.

For the members of Team Ten, the neighborhood as a social system was missing in this functional city; they based urban planning on anthropological aspects. In England, the MARS Group (Arthur Korn, Sigfried Giedion, Wells Coates, Maxwell Fry, 1933–1957), and in the Netherlands De 8 en Opbouw (1932–1943) supported a much more social approach. These ideas had a significant effect on urban planning and on individual buildings. Functional urban planning sought to use rows of terraced houses to implement the perfect lighting and ventilation conditions. It had long been an opponent of perimeter block developments. After 1945 they had won this debate and were able to build apartment houses in north-south orientation rows. Team Ten envisaged the buildings arranged in smaller and larger sub and main groups, turned towards each other to create neighborhoods, habitats, kasbahs or clusters. The model estate "Südliches Hansaviertel"

Hermann Hertzberger, Centraal Beheer in Apeldoorn, 1972
The offices of Centraal Beheer insurance company consist of 56 cubic elements. This workshop for 1,000 people offers an innovative open office concept with a wealth of informal meeting places in the building and on the roof top terraces.

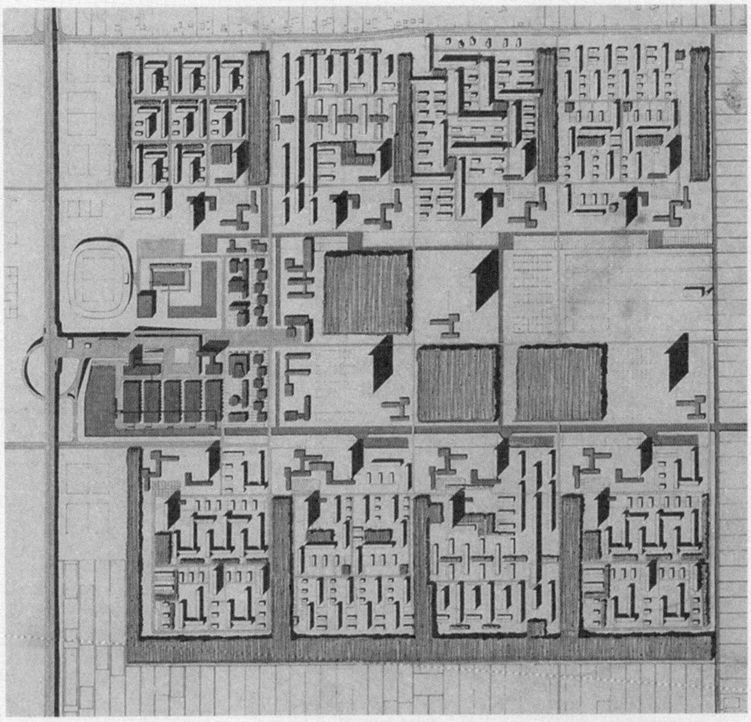

Jacob Bakema, presentation sheet for Alexanderpolder, 1956
In this neighborhood concept residents care for the communal gardens and extensive parks.

in Berlin by Otto Bartning was designed generally based on the CIAM principles of the separation of the four living environments listed above. It was built as part of the Interbau 1957 exhibition and demonstrated the idea of devising different types of buildings already separated into groups. In addition to numerous representatives of postwar Modernism, the well-known late brutalists Johannes van den Broek, Jacob Bakema, Hermann Fehling, Werner Düttmann and Paul Schneider-Essleben, among others, delivered plans for individual buildings. The implementation of this anthropological urban planning was only partially successful.

At the CIAM congress in La Sarraz in 1955, Jacob Bakema presented the new Alexanderpolder quarter in Amsterdam based on a grid system. The intention was that very different social and age groups should come together, accommodated in single-family houses and large-scale residential buildings, inspired by Le Corbusier's Unité: stacked one inside the other and ranging from large to small-scale building volumes. The practice of aligning all buildings parallel to each other largely disappeared and was only used in individual building groups. Megastructures bordered and divided the entire area. In the Smithson's Golden Lane plan, right angles were replaced with blunt angles, from which an open and irregular network of housing and streets in the air arose. In 1966, Kenzo Tange planned the reconstruction of Skopje, which had been destroyed by an earthquake. Based on Habitat 67, stacked city quarters were developed that included all the necessary infrastructure (shops, services), such as Wulfen Metacity, built in 1969 by Richard J. Dietrich and originally intended to be much larger (it was demolished in 1987). But mostly, the projects developed in the brutalist style remained true to the CIAM ideal with separation of functions and it was due to building costs that many more socially oriented ideas were not realized. The rows of continuous houses, propagated by CIAM were much cheaper – which was of course one of the intentions. Strongly worded criticism from the structuralist John Habraken was also aimed at this type of housing, rather than at the buildings in the brutalist tradition (largely due to the fact that they simply weren't so prevalent). Habraken lambasted his colleagues in 1961 in the book *The Supports and the People: The End of Mass Housing*, stating that architects are not artists and should not design buildings so freely. He demanded that the intended user participate in the building planning and that this participation should also include urban planning as a whole. However, two decades passed before the idea of participation was integrated into urban planning and, even today, this still isn't really effective.

This new understanding of working together arose in different degrees of private and public usage and even influenced the floor plans of the buildings: the new designs were laid out to encourage neighbors to meet each other, whether in Le Corbusier's "rues interieurs", or the Smithson's "Streets in the Sky"; these and other semi-public areas should be understood as belonging to everyone. Offices needed tea kitchens (Herman Hertzberger: Central Beheer in Apeldoorn) with bean bags (Xerox in Silicon Valley) and public buildings required informal meeting areas and internal streets as well as areas with undefined functions – such as the terraces discussed in the previous chapters. The Economist building by the Smithsons (chapter 4) – a design that proved a disappointment for Banham – dissolved the typical design of an office building, breaking what was usually one building into three separate volumes with a public piazza between them.

But this paradigm shift also influenced the private house. The identification with one's own house, the street, the cluster and finally the city began to play an important role once more. Dutch structuralism desired the further development of the built structure as a whole by the user and sought to design archetypal structures that represented a layered almost carpet-like order that is flexible enough to allow the user to change the order as desired. Such analytical observations arose as a result of Team Ten's Amsterdam magazine Forum, whose editorial office was taken over by Jacob Bakema and Aldo van Eyck in 1959. Van Eycks *The Story of a different Thought* included in the seventh edition in 1959 became the manifesto. The non-hierarchical relationships between elements or rooms became more important than the elements

Aldo van Eyck, Amsterdam Orphanage, 1960
Large two-story module in the foreground, small units in the background.

themselves. The first, and very typical example of this is the former orphanage, built by Aldo van Eyck in Amsterdam, 1959–1960: 328 small and eight large units with a quadratic floor plan create a flowing structure that opens out behind the long entrance area to form a number of inner courtyards. Every module comprises four round columns at the corners that support the pre-cast concrete domed roofs – the walls can be added or removed to create rooms of varying size. Both the open and openable (hatches) elements and the flexible floor plan (sliding walls) are typical of brutalist residential buildings. Even inner courtyards were extremely important for brutalist buildings, whether for the bungalows that followed the ancient Roman atrium house design, or as a closed private courtyard in large residential complexes, such as the terraced estate in Halen 1958–1962 by the Swiss architects Atelier 5, where a public village square with a number of multi-functional buildings served the community with communal areas, shops and a children's nursery.

Atelier 5, Halen Estate, 1961
Planting on roofs and in gardens make the terraced development a kind of hanging gardens.

Another typical feature of Brutalism is the introduction of greenery to the architecture. The architects built, for example, plant troughs into the building façades. This tradition can be seen in the terrace building in Halen, and in Tadao Ando's Rokko Housing in Kobe, 1981–1983, which can be considered either a late addition to the first phase of Brutalism, or the first example of the second phase.

Similar to the structuralists, the representatives of the Metabolism style in Japan also sought ways to redefine public and private space and to give society the spaces it required to unfold its true potential as part of a transformative process. The metabolists first came together at the CIAM in 1959 when Kenzo Tange presented two plans by Kiyonori Kikutake. For this group, the idea of growth and continuous change stood at the center of the exchange of the old for the new. Essentially, the idea was that small room modules should be fitted to a larger flexible structure and these were intended as replaceable elements. While Structuralism considered the private sphere just as important as the public sphere, Metabolism concentrated much more on the public sphere. A prime example of this is the Nakagin Capsule Tower by Kisho Kurokawa, 1970–1972, where the capsules served as exchangeable minimalist apartments.

Atelier 5, Halen Estate, 1961
The housing development near Berne, Switzerland comprises 81 privately owned houses arranged in three terraces.

by Charles Wright Architects

Stamp House

This luxury retreat and sanctuary is designed as a secure off-grid structure, carbon neutral in operation. The design hails the rise of a new tropical architecture of resilience, both brutal and elegant. The architects liked the idea that the concrete would develop a patina over time, further enhancing its sense of place in the environment. Critical aspects of the approach involved the development of new ways of living in tropical latitudes, providing secure yet flexible open areas for all functions including living, entertaining, dining, recreation and swimming. The main living areas oscillate around the central pool and landscaped courtyard, complemented by cascading waterfall features. The bedrooms are designed so that each has its own unique character by virtue of its orientation.

Location: Cape Tribulation, Australia
Architect: Charles Wright Architects
Year of Completion: 2013

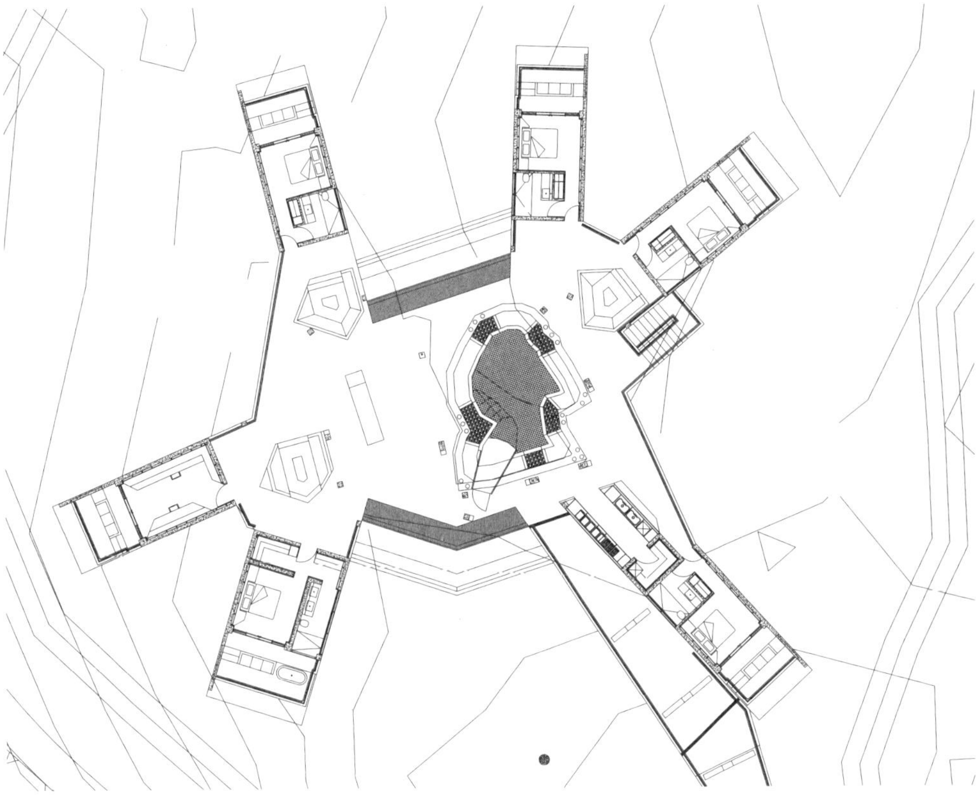

Floor plan level 1

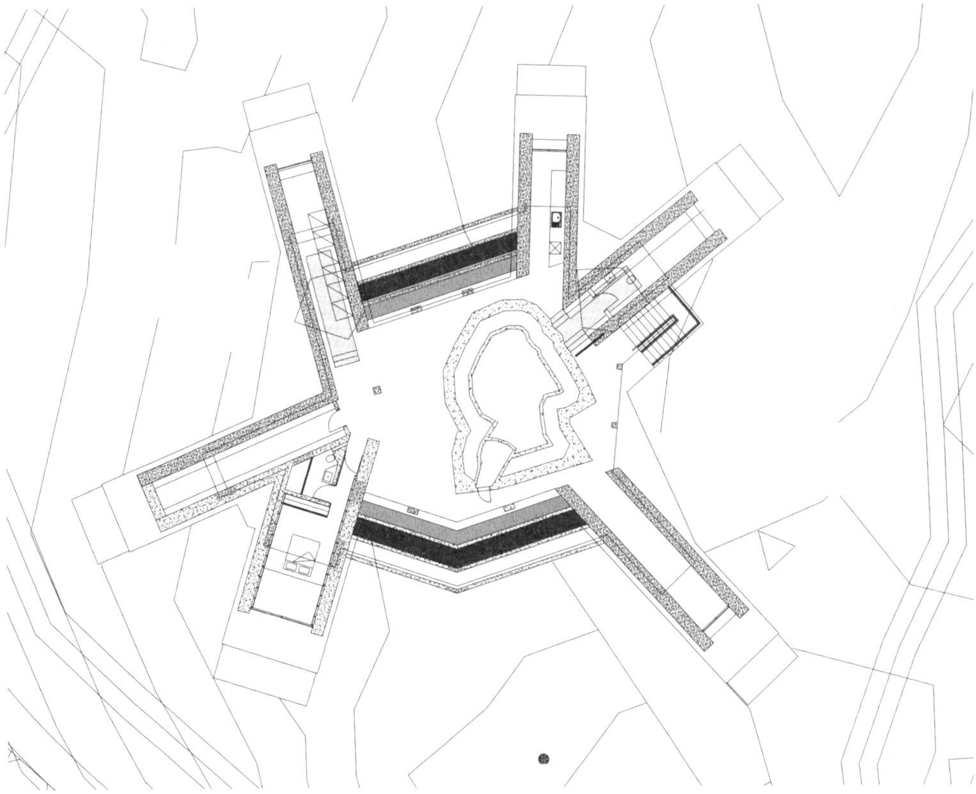

Floor plan undercroft

Open living spaces around central pool

View from lake

Covered terrace

Volume at night

Cantilevered building volume reflected in water

by Bak Gordon Arquitectos

Two Houses in Santa Isabel

Perhaps the most important aspect of this project is the desire to refer to the city within the city – interior areas formed by the street, square and block. This empty space was prominent in relation to the existing buildings; the vertical form of the façades contrasted the horizontal house. The architects have created a series of regular and hierarchical spaces, voids around which the required spaces for living gather. A first, more public, courtyard welcomes the residents and distributes them to the two houses. The houses have been built using exposed reinforced concrete and the boundaries will be covered with climbing plants, while the roof and other walls stay as they are. The spaces provide an illusion of positive and negative tensions, closed and open constructions that organize space.

Location: Santa Isabel, Lisbon, Portugal
Architect: Bak Gordon Arquitectos / Ricardo Bak Gordon
Year of Completion: 2010

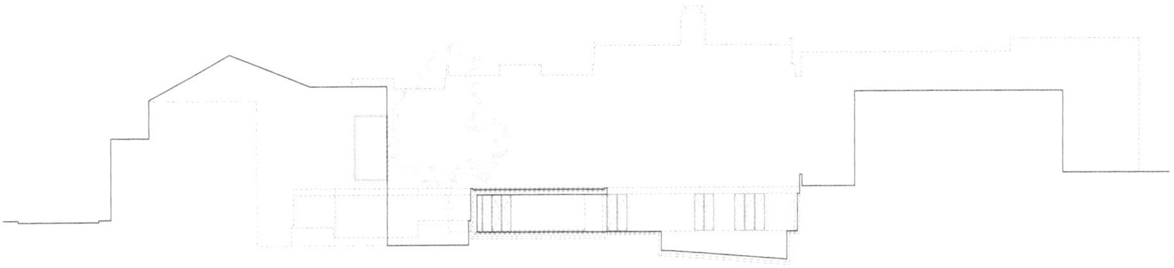

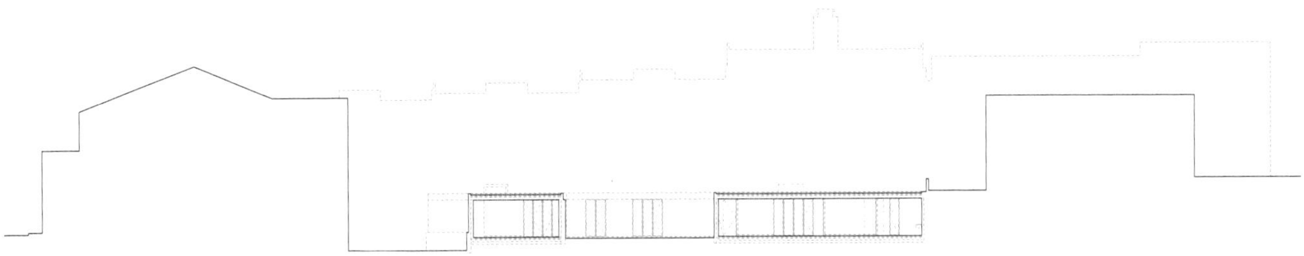

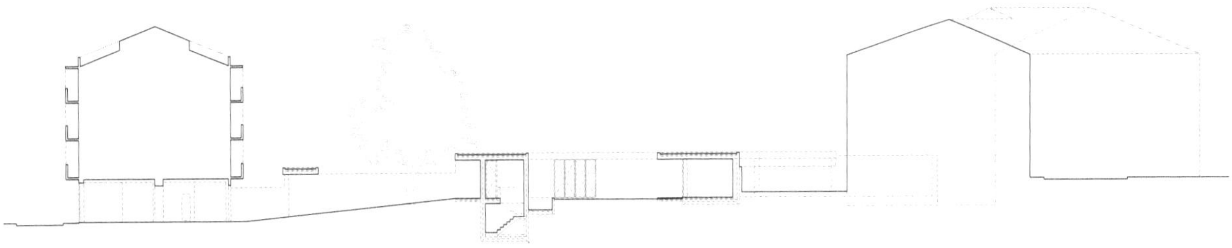

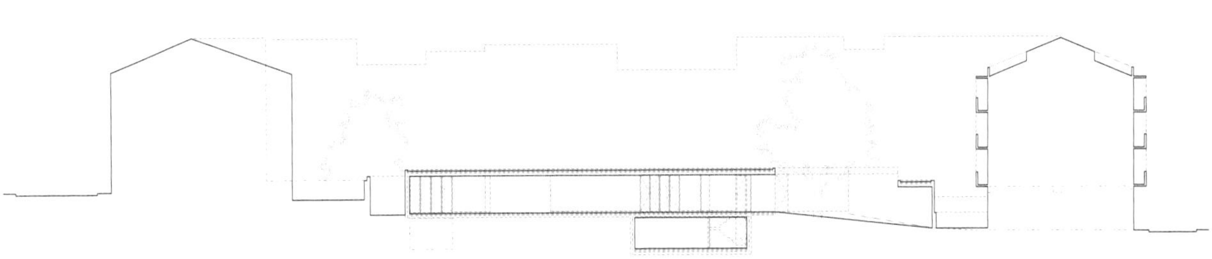

Sections

Concrete volume at night

Large glass doors contrast the solidity of the concrete

Living area with view of pool

Combination of voids, courtyards and architectural elements

by Renzo Piano Building Workshop

La Valletta City Gate

The City Gate project reconfigures the entrance to Valletta and comprises four parts: the Valletta City Gate and the square immediately outside the ramparts, the design of a theatre "machine" to be used for open-air productions in the ruins of the old opera house, the construction of a new Parliament building, and the re-landscaping of the moat. The bridge leading to the Valletta City Gate had been repeatedly enlarged over the years until it lost both its original function and proportions. The project restores the bridge to the dimensions of Dingli's original 1633 gate. Valletta's first city gate was probably a single tunnel through the city's ramparts. The initial objective of the project was therefore to reinstate the ramparts' original depth and strength. The architecture is very plain, giving the impression of power and austerity.

Location: La Valletta, Malta
Architect: Renzo Piano Building Workshop with Architecture Project (Valletta)
Year of Completion: 2015

The new city gate in the UNESCO World Heritage Site

Inside the new parliament building

The porous urban blocks of the city gate

View at night

Detail of the monolithic blocks

Inside the new parliament building

The volumetric blocks stand on slender columns

by Carlo Scarpa

Castelvecchio Museum

Carlo Scarpa's unique architectural style and sensitive approach to restoration design is made visible by the integration of old and new shown at the Castelvecchio, a red brick fortress originally built in the 14th century. After it was destroyed in World War II, it was carefully restored by Scarpa between 1959 and 1973 with many of his detailed designs mimicking the textures and forms of the Byzantine and Renaissance. Barrel vaults were replaced by wooden beams and cassette ceilings were complemented by concrete staircases and steel bridges. The dialogue between the old and new is further evident through expressed joints and cut-outs. Walls do not directly link to the floor but are expressed through an emphasized joint or break abruptly and act as cut-outs to present the visitor with changing views.

Location: Verona, Italy
Architect: Carlo Scarpa
Year of Completion: 1973

Steel bridges

New concrete stairs in old brick wall

Details emphasize the old and new structure

by Broissin

Green Hills Kindergarten

The Green Hills Kindergarten, located in the north of Mexico's metropolitan area, is a three-stage planned program, the first stage involved the kindergarten. The design is reminiscent of children's building blocks that have simply been left lying on the site. The prisms are playfully arranged and almost look as if they are trying to hide from one another. The concrete volumes tilt back and forth, motivating the children to explore and develop their creativity. The area for older children has a more linear design, and the simple construction is formed by reinforced concrete cradles supported on exposed concrete piles. This elevated condition, together with the slope of the terrain, favors the passage of rainwater below the building.

Location: Rancho San Juan, Ciudad López Mateos, Mexico
Architect: Broissin
Year of Completion: 2012

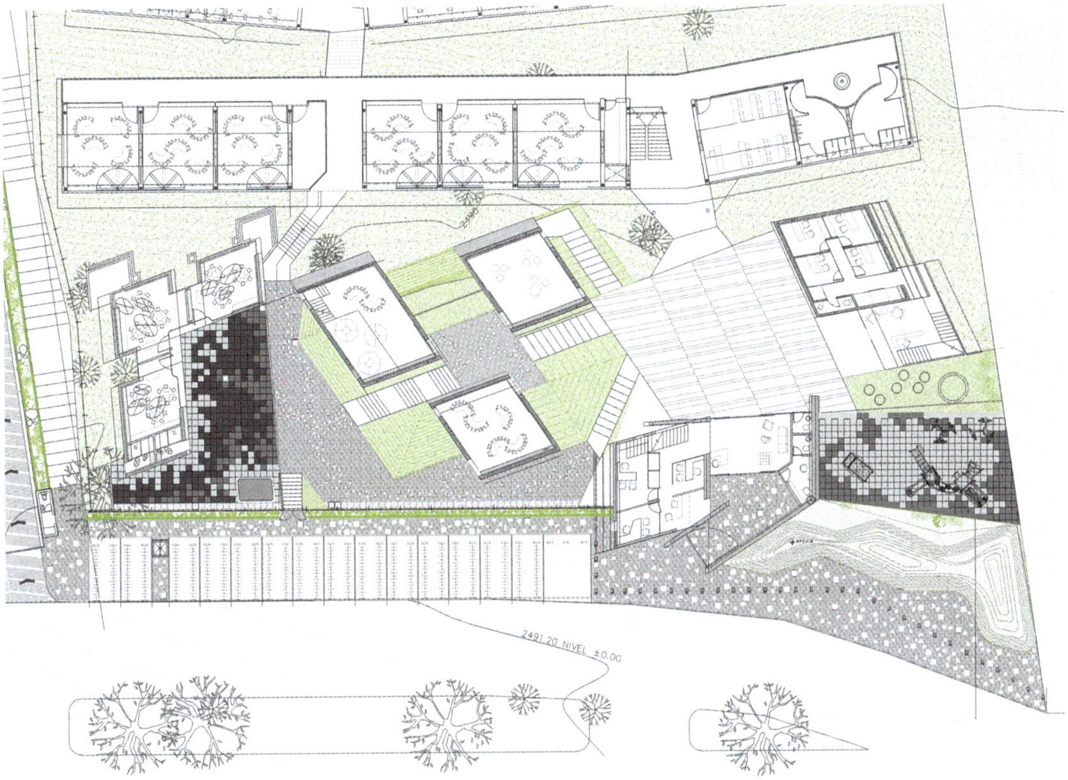

Site plan

Playfully arranged prisms

Main entrance area

Illuminated in the evening

Volumes connected by stairs and walkways

Combination of irregular round and square openings

Modern kindergarten interior

by Piet Bloom

Cube Houses

Houses like trees that fuse together to form a residential forest – this was the design idea behind this unusual concept for the Cube Houses by Dutch structuralist Piet Blom. The residents live in the "treetops", access is provided via the hexagonal, trunk comprising reinforced concrete columns and concrete blocks. Each of the 30 residential units comprises a cube with a length of 7.5 meters. Together these cubes form a coherent neighborhood. Each unit has three levels: living and dining areas, kitchen, office and a toilet are located on the lower floor, with two bedrooms and a bathroom on the middle level and a pyramid-shaped room with windows on the upper level.

Location: Rotterdam, The Netherlands
Architect: Piet Bloom
Year of Completion: 1984

Piled homes supported by hexagonal pylons

Entrance area

View of a neighborhood

by BAK arquitectos

Armenia Building

The Armenia Building is located in Palermo Soho, a neighborhood in the city of Buenos Aires. Due to the gentrification process that has occurred over the last decade, Palermo Soho has been renewed and has become a gastronomic, cultural, commercial and touristic hotspot, raising real estate prices in the area. In order to profit from the area's potential, an investment group commissioned an apartment building with a row of stores on the ground floor. The building comprises a varied set of apartments. While the commissioners intended most of them to be lofts that could be temporarily rented to tourists, the more spacious units – one, two, and three-bedroom apartments – would be sold as permanent residences. It was requested that the project would include common areas, green spaces, and a solarium.

Location: Palermo, Buenos Aires City, Argentina
Architects: BAK arquitectos / Besonías-Kruk
Year of Completion: 2016

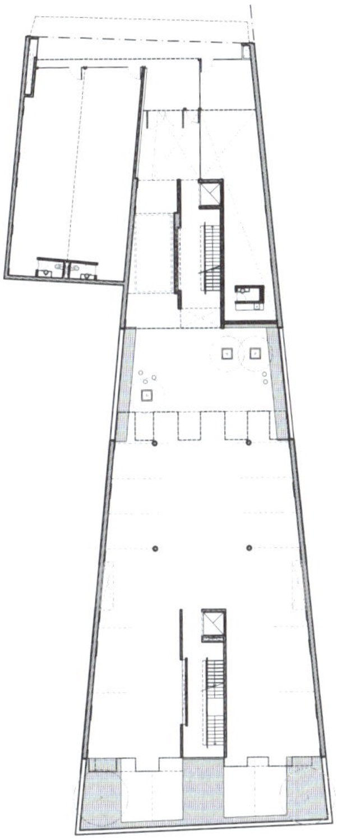

Ground floor

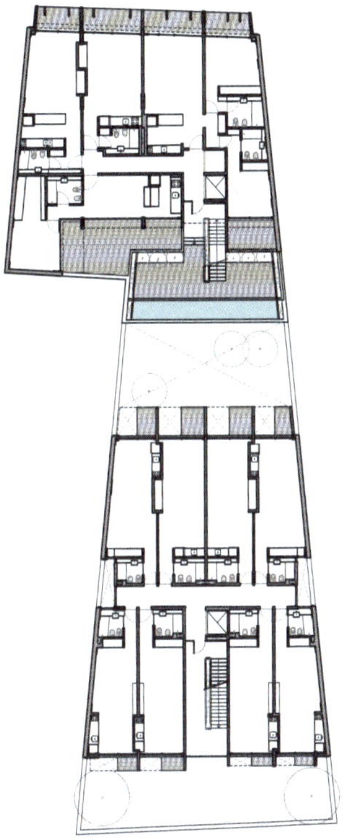

Second floor

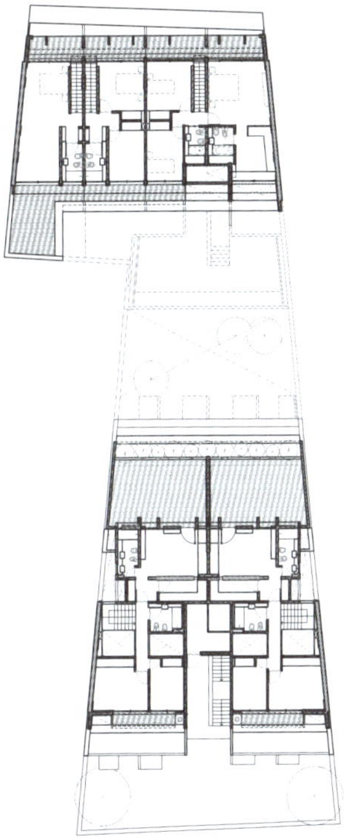

Fourth floor

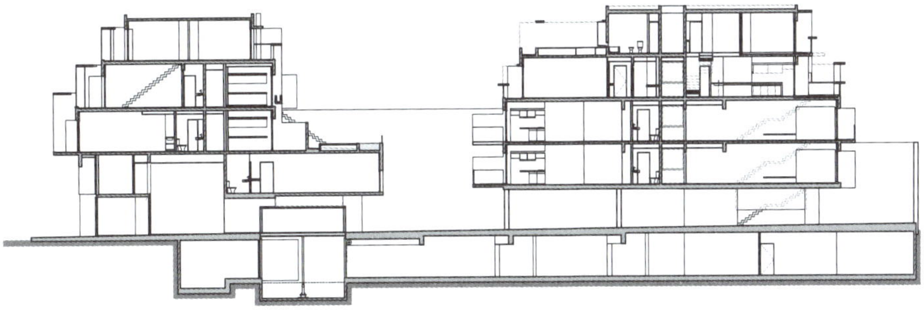

Section

Façade

Stairs

Corridor

Interior façade from solarium

Brise-soleils

Interior façade

by DnA_ Design And Architecture

Jinhua Architecture Park

Located in the Jinhua Architecture Park, an open space developed by Jinhua City government, this project was designed by renowned artist Ai Weiwei, and is one of 16 building projects located in the park, designed by international architects. This project is a public facility, divided into separate units and maximizing the privacy inside while minimizing land use in the park. The bent tube shape with an opening in the roof insures protection and privacy, as well as functional needs such as ventilation and natural lighting. This layout allows flexible reproduction in the park to suit future needs. The quirky volumes have an interesting esthetic, encouraging a smile from passersby and appearing almost like snorkels rising from the landscape, giving the impression they could sink back down and disappear at any moment.

Location: Jinhua, China
Architect: DnA_Design And Architecture
Year of Completion: 2006

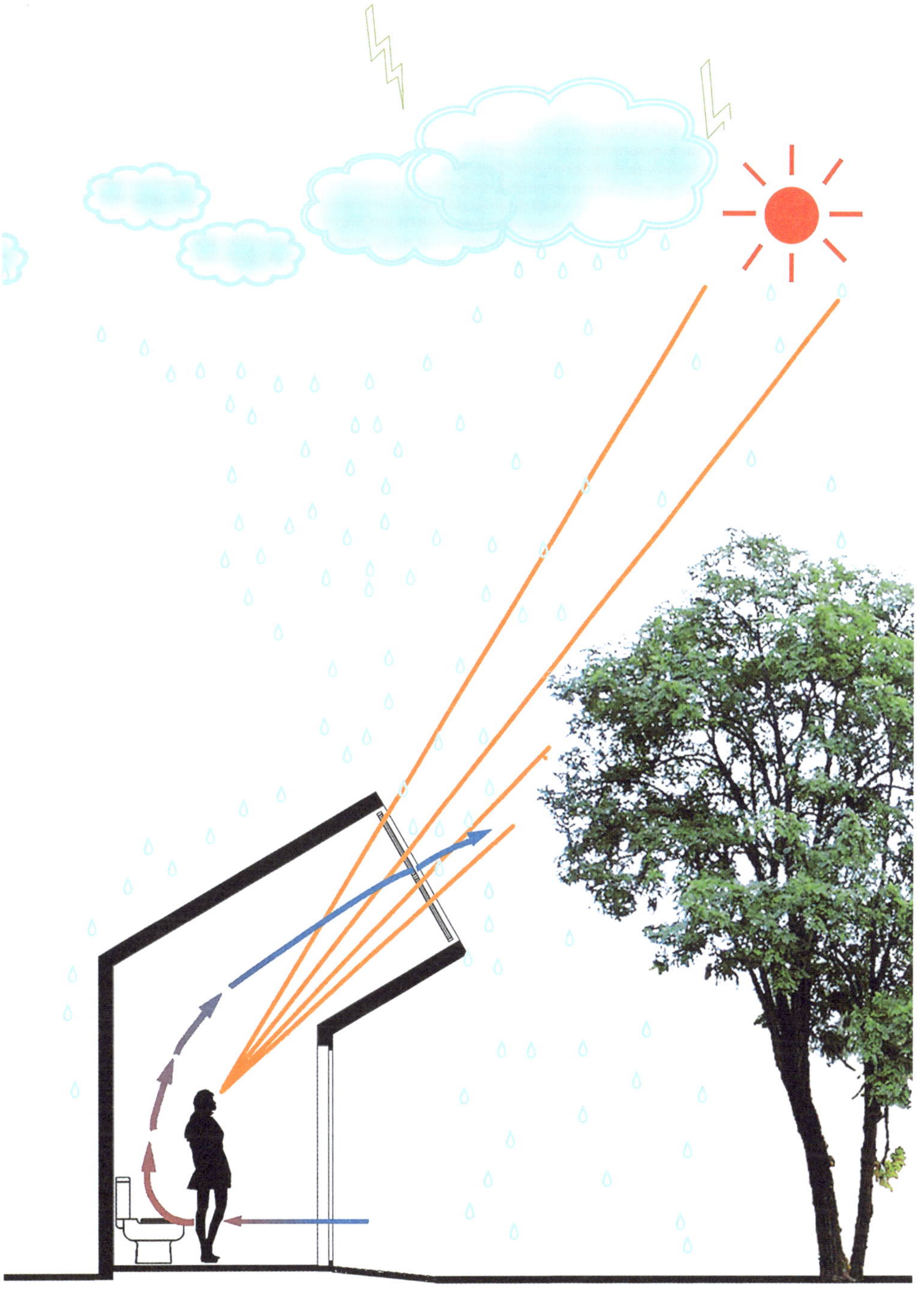

Sunlight and ventilation diagram

Opening lets in light and air while maintaining privacy

Individual constructions grouped together

Arrangement means that the units are separate and yet unified

Volumes give the impression they are looking away from each other to ensure privacy

by Gérard Grandval

Cabbages of Créteil

These ten cylindrical residential buildings, each 15 stories in height, look like large plants from another world. They are known as Les Choux (the cabbages), due to the unusual shape of their balconies. Sometimes the towers are also referred to as dahlias, corn cobs, or flower houses. The curvaceous concrete petal-shaped balconies provide plenty of private outdoor space for the occupants. They were intended to be similar to gardens. Wooden shutters provide an interesting material contrast. The Paris suburb of Créteil, where the towers were built, was formerly a cabbage field – and perhaps that was the source of the architect's inspired design. Grandval hated cubes, saying they were "too clean, without mystery" – his homes are therefore dynamic, vegetal forms and very much anti-cube.

Location: Créteil, France
Architect: Gérard Grandval
Year of Completion: 1974

Detail of balconies

Cabbage-like appearance

Three of the ten towers

by Pezo von Ellrichshausen

Guna House

Hemmed in between a steeply sloping hillside and a wood of eucalyptus trees, this house offers stunning views over the surrounding landscape. A monolithic prism of concrete attempts to articulate the contradictions of the topography with a square top floor measuring 20 meters on each side and balanced on top of a compact lower story measuring 8.5 meters on each side. The upper floor is a dogmatic piano nobile that compensates for the inconvenience of the diagonally set natural slope of the terrain, based on a grid of four modules on each side. The middle rooms on each side face a central patio, while those at the corners are articulated by circulations that occupy a subsidiary module. The bottom floor houses the more day-to-day functions of the domestic realm. The four walls of the patio act as Vierendeel girders resting in balance on the podium.

Location: San Pedro de la Paz, Chile
Architect: Pezo von Ellrichshausen
Year of Completion: 2014

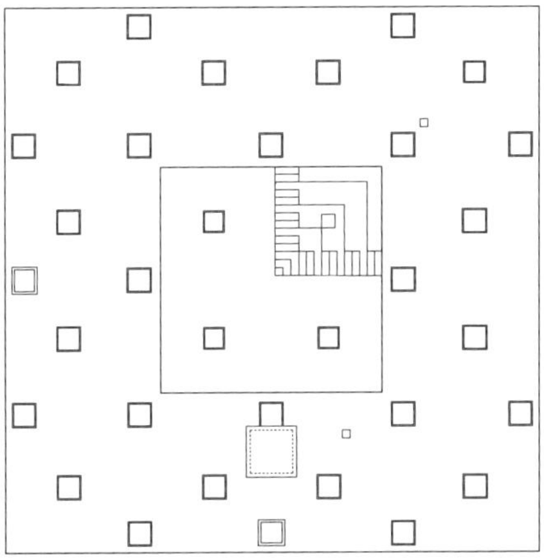

Roof plan

Upper floor plan

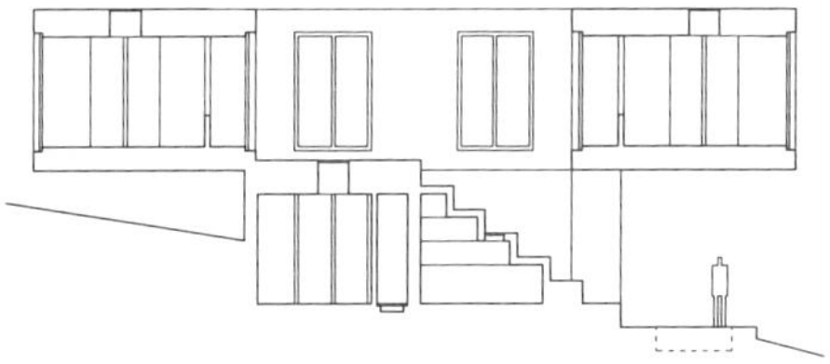

Section

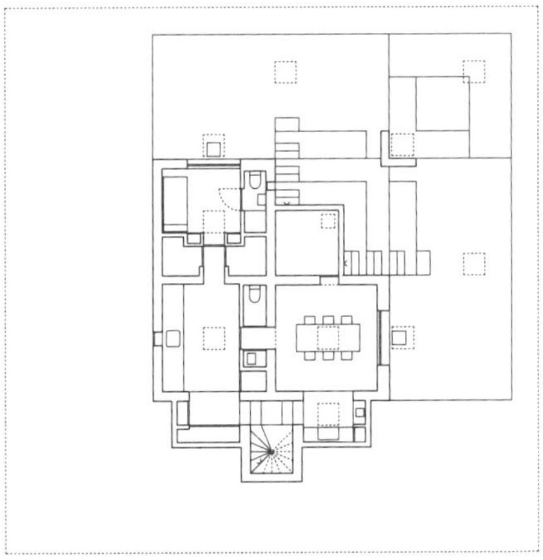

Lower floor plan

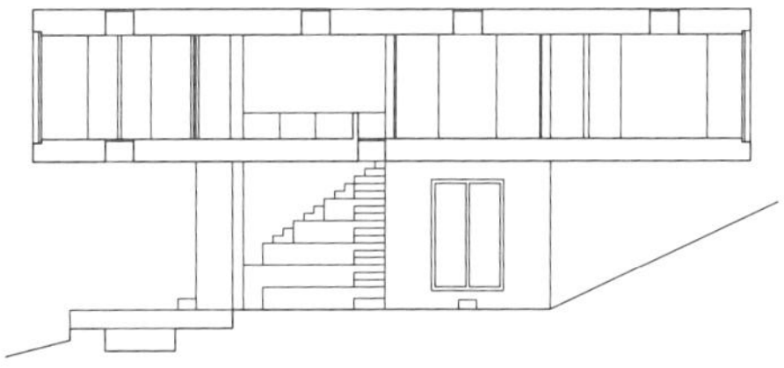

Section

View to the lagoon from lower ground floor

Interior circulation path

Concrete steps to central patio

Solid concrete steps

Central patio

Building set into the slope and surrounded by trees

Building offers stunning views of the surroundings

by Kisho Kurokawa

Nakagin Capsule Tower

This mixed-use residential and office building comprises two interconnected concrete towers housing 140 self-contained prefabricated capsules. The capsules were fitted with pre-assembled interior features such as a circular window, a built-in bed and a bathroom, before being shipped to the building site where they were attached to the concrete core using just four high-tension bolts for each unit. This means that the units can be easily replaced. Each capsule measures 2.3 × 3.8 × 2.1 meters. They can be connected and combined to create larger spaces. The capsules are all welded lightweight steel truss boxes clad in galvanized, rib-reinforced steel panels. Nakagin Capsule Tower is a rare remaining example of Japanese Metabolism, an architectural movement emblematic of Japan's postwar cultural resurgence.

Location: Tokyo, Japan
Architect: Kisho Kurokawa
Year of Completion: 1972

General view

Circular window

View from below

by Valentiny hvp architects

Schengen School Complex

This large school complex serves the community of Schengen and is located at the edge of the village in a rural setting. The two buildings have been composed so that the spaces between and around the constructions fuse together to form a free-flowing space. The covered entrance areas and wide roof overhangs help to smooth the transition between inside and outside. Inside, the design offers sweeping views of the surrounding countryside on one side, and internal views on the other side. The classrooms are organized in pairs with space between. On the ground floor, the ceiling is made of pre-fabricated components and has an almost vault-like appearance. The concrete façade is made of poured concrete, while the interior makes use of exposed concrete.

Location: Remerschen, Luxembourg
Architect: Valentiny hvp architects
Year of Completion: 2003

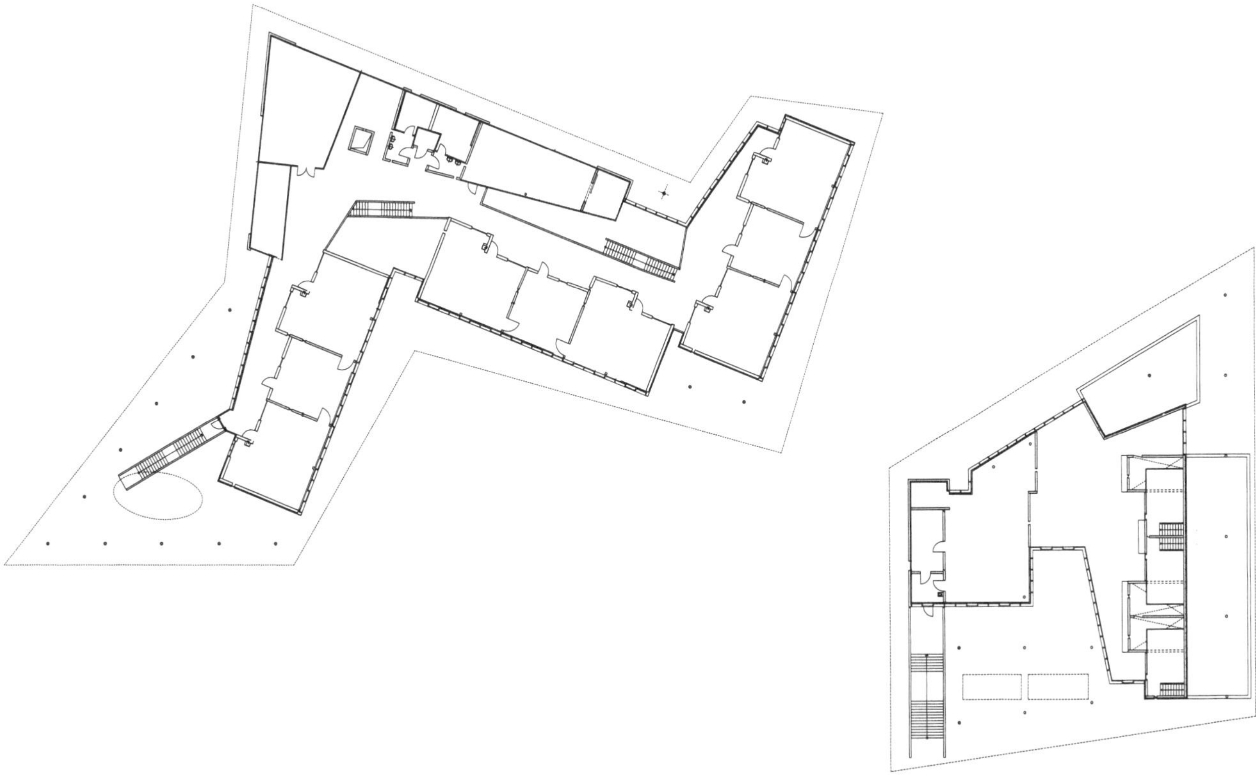

Upper floor plan

Ground floor plan

Outdoor facilities

Corridor primary school

Entrance to primary school

Concrete façade kindergarten

Stairs to kindergarten

View at night

by VTN architects

House for Trees

As a result of rapid urbanization, cities in Vietnam have diverged far from their origins as sprawling tropical forests. In Ho Chi Minh City, for example, only 0.25 percent of the entire city is covered with greenery. An over-abundance of motorbikes causes daily traffic congestion as well as serious air pollution. House for Trees is an effort to change this situation. The aim is to reintroduce greenery to the city, introducing big tropical trees into areas of high-density dwellings. Five concrete boxes have been designed as "pots" to plant trees on top of the living spaces. With a thick layer of soil, these pots also function as storm water basins for retention and therefore help to reduce the risk of flooding. The idea is envisioned to be employed on large number of houses in the future.

Location: Tan Binh district, Ho Chi Minh City, Vietnam
Architect: VTN architects
Year of Completion: 2014

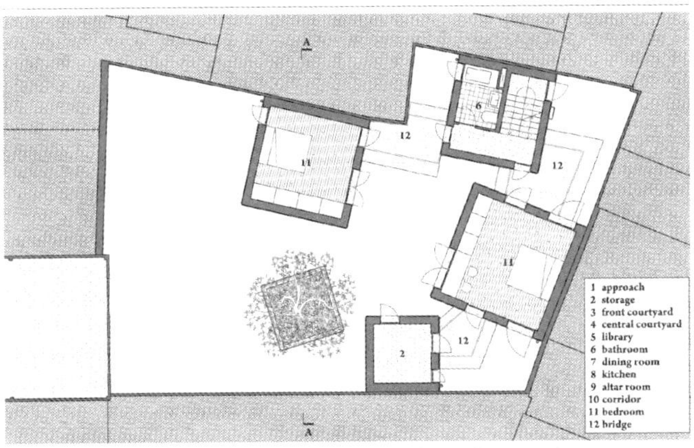

First floor plan

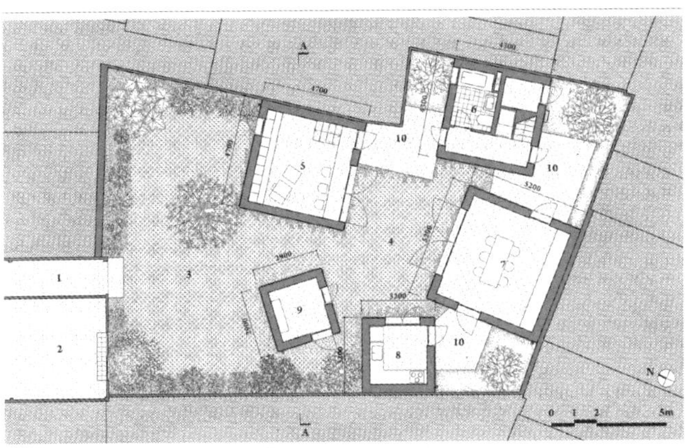

Ground floor plan

Elevation

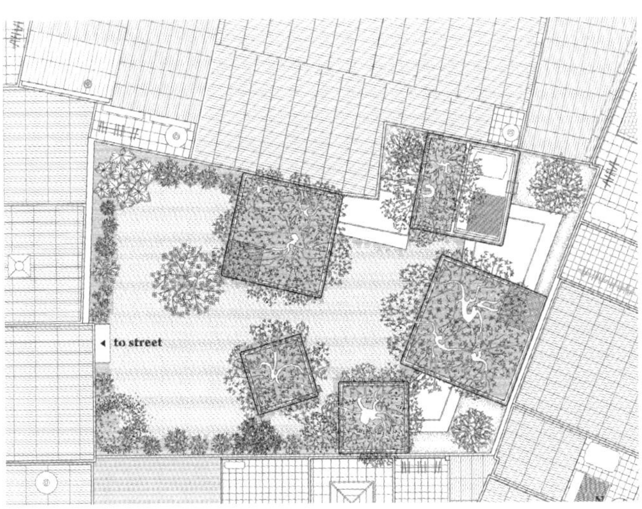

Site plan

Section

Open courtyard

Courtyard between trees

Closed view from outside

Communicative units inside the complex

Closed walls on the outside

Brick interiors

Brutalism Now and Then

"Brutalism nearly always uses concrete at its roughest (Béton brut) with overemphasis on big chunky members which collide ruthlessly." This is the definition given in the 1999 edition of the *Dictionary of Architecture & Landscape Architecture* by Pevsner, Honour and Fleming. If Brutalism was the typical stylistic expression of the Cold War era (Beanland, p. 16), then it, fortunately, could be considered a thing of the past. Brutalism might not have ended so suddenly and not in the 1960s, like Banham suggests, or even on one particular day in 1972 as Jencks claims, but it did ebb in the late 1970s, and even before the end of the Cold War it was forced to make way for high-tech solutions and, above all, the Post-Modern style.

That this return to classical proportions and formulations arose may even have been predicted by Banham when he dismissed the work of Oswald Mathias Ungers due to the historical, rather than brutalist, character of his buildings. What would today be termed as flaming soon began to surround Brutalism, the likes of which had only been seen before in the belligerent response of representatives of the Classical Modern to historical buildings of the late 19th century. The heavily criticized growth of urban development and high-rise buildings resulted in the use of concrete being largely abandoned, particularly exposed aggregate concrete. In the same way that Brutalism accused the glass and steel modern style of working with the wrong materials and ignoring the

Tadao Ando, Rokko Housing, Kobe, 1983
Terraced housing as starting point of the second wave of Brutalism.

needs of the users, Brutalism now found itself being charged with the exact same offense. Earlier even the Eiffel Tower fell victim to accusations of this kind, as did the high-tech Centre Georges Pompidou.

Prince Charles became one of the most important critics of Brutalism, despite the fact that it was a style founded in his homeland. His plans for Poundbury, devised with Léon Krier, are similar to Disney's Celebration and an example of a romantic New Urbanism.

During this era, but on the other side of the iron curtain, the creation of a pure form of Brutalism was still taking place. Although it

Enric Miralles and Carme Pinos: Igualada Cemetry, Barcelona, 1994
Exposed prefab concrete meets free formed gabions.

began much later than in the West – after the death of Stalin and the official end of Socialist Realism in 1955. It took a while for the countries behind the curtain to catch up with developments in the West. The amount of time it took to build anything in the Eastern Bloc meant that numerous buildings conceived in the 1970s were only completed in the mid or late 1980s. There Brutalism continued until the fall of the Berlin wall in 1989 and it was at this point that Brutalism began to make its return in the West – not that it ever completely died out – as seen in Tadao Ando's Rokko Housing in Kobe (1983), Peter Märkli's house La Congiunta (1992) and Wiel Arets's Pension Fund in Heerlen (1995). The works of various architects, such as Álvaro Siza Vieira or Paulo Mendes da Rocha even sought to bridge the stylistic gap between the first and second waves of Brutalism. Even in Africa, the Arabian Peninsula, and Central and Southeast Asia, massive exposed concrete buildings never truly disappeared. The same applies for the use of exposed technical installations as a stylistic technique. This is not discussed in this book, but could reasonably be considered an important criterion, beginning with Le Corbusier's Unité, but also implemented in his church building in Ronchamp. Nowadays, building regulations often don't allow this strategy.

In the case of prominent architecture, concrete was able to quickly make a comeback in the form of a fine, almost velvety surfaces as seen in Tadao Ando's buildings for example. Imprints from the formwork and exposed aggregate concrete have only recently began to gain in popularity again. Non-precious corten steel is also extremely popular. An un-Palladian structure is now present everywhere since the Post-Modern and classical structures began to die out. Although this is surely different to how Banham imagined it; his "image" has returned in the form of BLOb and Fold Architecture, which started picking up on the brutalist style once more.

Architects Index

Picture Credits

(AUT)side
flickr.com
(page 31 b.)
AlfvanBeem
Wikimedia Commons
(page 110 b.)
Alwikiuser
Wikimedia Commons
(page 128 a.)
Anagoria
Wikimedia Commons
(pages 204 b., 205)
Apdency
Wikimedia Commons
(page 240)
Fai Au
(pages 98–101)
Raphael Azevedo Franca
Wikimedia Commons
(page 294)
Iwan Baan
(pages 8, 191–193,
232 a., 233 b.)
Banalities
Wikimedia Commons
(pages 40, 41 a.)
Sachin Bandukwala, Ahmedabad
(pages 207–209)
Bozo Benic
(page 32)
Bigjap
Wikimedia Commons
(page 69)
Patrick Bingham-Hall
(pages 8, 246, 248–251)
Jan Bitter, Berlin
(pages 164, 166–167)
Jonhy Blaze
flickr.com
(page 72)
Roman Boed
Wikimedia Commons
(page 96 a. l.)
Simone Bossi
(pages 54, 56–57)
Timothy Brown
Wikimedia Commons
(page 126)
Barbara Bühler
(pages 80–81, 82 b. r.)
Tamás Bujnovszky
(pages 48, 50–51)
Hardy Buob
(page 82 a.)
Alex Buob
(pages 82 b. l., 83 a., 83 b.)
Lionel CLOT
Wikimedia Commons
(pages 152–153)
Simon Constantini
(pages 113, 114 a., 115a.)
Daderot
Wikimedia Commons
(pages 20–21, 175 b., 182,
214–215)
Jean-Pierre Dalbéra
Wikimedia Commons
(pages 111, 228 a. l., 228 b. l.)
Luis Dantas
Wikimedia Commons
(page 71)
Michel Denancé
(pages 256–259)

Design And Architecture, Beijing
(pages 272, 274–275)
Vincent Desjardin
Wikimedia Commons
(pages 5, 97)
vincent desjardins
flickr.com
(pages 9, 228 b. r., 229)
Elins
Pixabay
(page 84 a. r.)
F.Eveleens
Wikimedia Commons
(page 267 a.)
Field Condition, New York City
(pages 224 b., 227 b.)
first365
Pixabay
(page 84 a. r.)
Paul Fleury
Wikimedia Commons
(pages 276–277)
Foto Tappeiner
(pages 114 b. r., 114 b. l., 115 b.)
Pedro França / Agência Senado
Wikimedia Commons
(page 102 b.)
Zdeněk Fránek
(pages 26, 28–29)
Naoya Fuji
Wikimedia Commons
(page 186)
Marc Gerritsen
(pages 231, 233 a.)
Sergio Ghetti
(pages 60 a., 61 a. r.)
giggel
Wikimedia Commons
(page 19)
Dennis Gilbert
VIEW/ARTUR IMAGES
(page 11)
Ginkgo2g
Wikimedia Commons
(pages 243–245)
Gabriele Giuseppini
Wikimedia Commons
(page 266)
Gobierno de la Ciudad de Buenos Aires
Wikimedia Commons
(page 53 b.)
Tim Gouw punttim
Wikimedia Commons
(page 267 b. r.)
Fernando Guerra | FG+SG
(pages 252, 254–255)
Eduardo Gulot
flickr.com
(page 15)
Bobak Ha'Eri
Wikimedia Commons
(page 73)
Hannes Henz, Zurich
(pages 22–25)
Het Nieuwe Instituut
Flickr.com
(pages 128 b., 241)
Carol M. Highsmith / Library of Congress
Wikimedia Commons
(pages 16, 74–75, 96 l. b, 146, 147 a., 222–223)
Tony Hisgett
Wikimedia Commons
(pages 124, 129)
Ivory
Wikimedia Commons
(page 267 b. l.)
jackmac34
Pixabay
(page 181)
Jules & Jenne
flickr.com
(pages 64, 65 b.)
jv.resolution
www.flickr.com
(page 261 a. r.)
Kecko
Wikimedia Commons
(page 127)
Casey Kelbaugh
(pages 4, 119)
GG Kirchner
(pages 286, 288–289)
Kiwiev
Wikimedia Commons
(page 12)

H. Kopp
flickr.com
(pages 30, 31 a. l., 298 b. l.)
Shin Kyungsub
(pages 217–221)
Bryan Ledgard
Wikimedia Commons
(page 85)
LucEdouard
flickr.com
(page 14)
Habib M'henni
Wikimedia Commons
(pages 162, 297 r.)
Daniela Mac Adden
(pages 268, 270–271)
Graeme Maclean
Wikimedia Commons
(pages 41 b. r., 41 b. l.)
Tomáš Malý
(pages 104–107, 297 l.)
Man vyi
Wikimedia Commons
(page 116 a. r.)
Mdbeckwith
Wikimedia Commons
(page 116 b.)
Menis Arquitectos
(page 34 a.)
Matthew Millman, San Francisco
(pages 36–39)
Harry Mitchell
Wikimedia Commons
(pages 163 a., 163 b. l.)
paulisson miura
Wikimedia Commons
(pages 62–63)
Musikfan-RMS
Wikimedia Commons
(page 163 b. r.)
Jaime Navarro
(pages 154, 156 a.,
156 b. l., 157 a.)
Nesnad
Wikimedia Commons
(pages 285 a. l., 285 b.)
Leandro Neumann Ciuffo
Wikimedia Commons
(page 96 a. r.)
Axel Nieberg
(pages 148–151)
Nizio Design International
(pages 200–203)
Nicolas Nova
Wikimedia Commons
(pages 6, 136)
Hiroyuki Oki
(pages 8, 290, 292–293)
Marcos Oliveira/ Agência Senado
Wikimedia Commons
(pages 188–189)
Andrea Osti
www.flickr.com
(pages 260, 298 l. a.)
Pillar Pedreira / Agência Senado
Wikimedia Commons
(page 103)
Alex Pereira
Wikimedia Commons
(page 102 a. r.)
Sandra Pereznieto
(pages 210–213)
Pezo von Ellrichshausen
(pages 278, 280–283)
Filippo Poli
(pages 168, 170–173, 298 r.)
Andreas Praefcke
Wikimedia Commons
(page 184)
Evelyn Proimos
Wikimedia Commons
(page 53 a.)
Alex Proimos
Wikimedia Commons
(page 84 a. l.)
Bharath Ramamrutham
(pages 58, 59 b., 60 b.,
61 a. l., 61 b.)
Reading Tom
Wikimedia Commons
(page 187)
Christian Richters
(pages 133 b., 134 b. r.,
134 b. l., 135 b.)
Alexandre de la Roche
(pages 262–265)
rokker
Wikimedia Commons
(page 137 a.)

Ralf Roletschek
Wikimedia Commons
(page 127)
Fred Romero
Flickr.com
(pages 4, 185, 228 a. r.)
Rosenthal, James W., creator / Library of Congress
Wikimedia Commons
(pages 130–131)
Piergiorgio Rossi
Wikimedia Commons
(page 295)
Simona Rota
(pages 34 b. l., 34 b. r., 35 a., 35 b.)
rtlinfo
Pixabay
(page 180)
Roque de Sá / Agência Senado
Wikimedia Commons
(page 102 a. l.)
Koji Sakai, Hokkaido
(page 161)
JC Sancho Osinaga
(pages 236 a., 236 b., 237 b.)
Ibone Santiago
Wikimedia Commons
(page 70 b.)
sarahmirk
Wikimedia Commons
(page 175 a.)
Fumiaki Sato, Hokkaido
(pages 158, 160)
Jonathan Savoie
Wikimedia Commons
(page 16)
seier+seier
Wikimedia Commons
(pages 90–91, 194–195)
seier+seier
www.flickr.com
(pages 17, 261 b.)
Eduardo Selva
(pages 142, 144–145)
Shaqspeare / Unify
Wikimedia Commons
(page 204 a. l.)
Su Shengliang
(pages 138–139, 140 b., 141)
Jessica Sheridan
Wikimedia Commons
(pages 147 b. l., 147 b. r.)
Sigurgeir Sigurjónsson
(pages 92–95)
Silenceisfoo
Wikimedia Commons
(page 70 a.)
Sophus Søbye
(page 177 b.)
Wladyslaw Sojka / www.sojka.photo
Wikimedia Commons
(pages 108–109, 238)
Gustavo Sosa Pinilla
(pages 42, 44–47)
Spaceshift Studio, Bangkok
(pages 86–89)
Steffen Stamp
(pages 176, 178 a., 178 b. r., 178 b. l., 179 a., 179 b.)
Studio Zhu-Pei
(pages 232 b. r., 232 b. l.)
Esteban Suarez
(pages 155 a., 155 b., 156 b. r., 157 b.)
NamGoong Sun
(pages 77–79)
Ben Sutherland
(page 65 a.)
Hisao Suzuki
(pages 235, 237 a. l., 237 a. r.)
Sweetie candykim
Wikimedia Commons
(page 117)
Tamorlan
Wikimedia Commons
(page 18)
Taxiarchos228
Wikimedia Commons
(page 204 a. l.)
Diego Terna
Wikimedia Commons
(page 242)
Aleksandrs Timofejevs
Wikimedia Commons
(page 52)
Tktktk
Wikimedia Commons
(page 174)

University of Liverpool Faculty of Health & Life Sciences
flickr.com
(page 116 a. l.)
urbzoo
Wikimedia Commons
(pages 284, 285 a. r.)
Chris van Uffelen
(pages 7, 66)
AlfvanBeem
Wikimedia Commons
(page 110 b.)
Albert Vecerka / Esto, New York City
(pages 225–226, 227 a.)
Guilhem Vellut
Wikimedia Commons
(page 110 a.)
Gonzalo Viramonte
(pages 197–199)
Lukas Wassmann /
Totalworld.com
(pages 120–123)
Esther Westerveld
flickr.com
(page 68)
YKah
Wikimedia Commons
(page 137 b.)
Zemlinki!
www.flickr.com
(page 261 a. l.)
Yohan Zerdoun
(pages 132, 134 a., 135 a.)
Xia Zhi
(page 140 a.)
Zyxwodron
pixelio.de
(page 31 a. r.)

Cover front (from above to below): Fritz Wotruba; Foldes Architects; William Pereira
Cover back: Lina Bo Bardi

Imprint

The Deutsche Nationalbibliothek lists this publication in the Deutsche Nationalbibliografie; detailed bibliographic data are available on the Internet at http://dnb.dnb.de

ISBN 978-3-03768-224-1

www.braun-publishing.ch

2nd edition 2022

Editor: Editorial Office van Uffelen
Editorial staff and layout: Susanne Bauer, Lisa Rogers, Georgia van Uffelen, Celine Zaiser
Graphic concept: Ultrapaper – creative Studio
Reproduction: Bild1Druck GmbH, Berlin